U0875917

中国思想文化术语多语种对外翻译标准化建设项目成果

CHINESE THINKING AND CULTURE MULTILINGUAL TERMINOLOGY DATABASE

中华源·河南故事

CHINESE CIVILIZATION
Stories from Henan

黄河流域高质量发展

HIGH-QUALITY DEVELOPMENT OF THE YELLOW RIVER BASIN

河南省人民政府外事办公室 编

河南大学出版社
HENAN UNIVERSITY PRESS
·郑州·

图书在版编目（CIP）数据

中华源·河南故事．黄河流域高质量发展 ：汉英对照 / 河南省人民政府外事办公室编．-- 郑州 ：河南大学出版社，2023.7

ISBN 978-7-5649-5543-4

Ⅰ．①中… Ⅱ．①河… Ⅲ．①地方文化－河南－通俗读物－汉、英②黄河流域－流域经济－区域经济发展－通俗读物－汉、英 Ⅳ．①G127.61-49 ②F127.2-49

中国国家版本馆CIP数据核字（2023）第122538号

黄河流域高质量发展

HUANGHE LIUYU GAOZHILIANG FAZHAN

责任编辑 李亚涛 屈琳玉

责任校对 柳 涛

封面设计 翟淼淼

版式设计 李雪艳

出版发行 河南大学出版社

地址：郑州市郑东新区商务外环中华大厦2401号 邮编：450046

电话：0371-86059701（营销部）

0371-86059750（高等教育与职业教育分公司）

网址：hupress.henu.edu.cn

排　　版 河南大学出版社设计排版部

印　　刷 河南华彩实业有限公司

版　　次 2023年7月第1版　　**印　　次** 2023年7月第1次印刷

开　　本 710 mm×1010 mm 1/16　　**印　　张** 12

字　　数 236千字　　**定　　价** 57.00元

中华源·河南故事·黄河流域高质量发展

主　　编　刘炯天

副 主 编　刘建华

中文撰稿　张　伟　张晓昱　王慧扬

英文译者　张庆彬　李　洁　陈行洁　屈璟峰

英文审校　Marc van Rossem

Chinese Civilization
Stories from Henan
Grain of the Central Plains

Editor-in-Chief	Liu Jiongtian
Associate Editor-in-Chief	Liu Jianhua
Writers	Zhang Wei Zhang Xiaoyu Wang Huiyang
Translators	Zhang Qingbin Li Jie Chen Xingjie Qu Jingfeng
Translation Proofreader	Marc van Rossem

总 序

中国是世界四大文明古国之一，也是世界上唯一的古代文明传统未曾中断的国家。河南省地处中国中东部，是中华文明和中华民族的重要发祥地，在中国五千年的文明史上，河南作为国家政治、经济、文化的中心就长达三千多年。从某种意义上讲，一部河南史就是半部中国史。这里是中华人文始祖黄帝的故乡，是古丝绸之路的东方起点，是少林功夫和陈氏太极的发源地，这里创建了中国历史上最早的都城，镌刻了中国最古老的文字，诞生了中国最初的商业文明。

伴随着新时代的荣光，河南经济社会发展迅速，人民生活水平显著提升，这是河南人民自力更生、艰苦奋斗的历史结果，也是对外开放带来的益处。河南经济社会的发展、人民生活方式的改变都植根于深层次的文化积淀。为了让世界更多地了解河南，让河南更好地走向世界，2018年以来，河南省人民政府外事办公室认真研析了这片古老土地上的历史文化资源和时代风貌，组织各领域权威专家学者，编译了“中华源·河南故事”中外文系列丛书，选取黄河文化、河洛文化、老子、庄子、黄帝、少林功夫、太极拳、中医、汉字、丝绸之路、古都、农业、大运河、文物、陶瓷、青铜器、手工艺、书法、杂技、豫菜、豫剧、脱贫攻坚、空中丝绸之路、航空城、南水北调、中原粮谷、红旗渠、焦裕禄等多个主题，力图以故事的方式向世界展现一个立体、全面、真实的河南。

当今世界，人类文明无论是在物质还是在精神方面都取得了巨大进步，特别是物质的极大丰富，这在古代世界是完全不能想象的。同时，当代人类也面临着许多突出的难题，比如，贫富差距持续扩大，物欲追求奢华无度，个人主义恶性膨胀，社会诚信不断消减，伦理道德每况愈下，人与自然关系日趋紧张，等等。要解决这些难题，不仅需要运用人类今天的智慧和力量，而且需要运用人类历史上积累和储存的智慧和力量。河南历史文化底蕴深厚、包容性强，在今天仍极具现实意义。中原文化蕴含的思想智慧有助于修身养性，推动人类社会进步发展，焦裕禄精神、红旗渠精神所体现的为民爱民、艰苦奋斗的价值取向是构建人类命运共同体的力量源泉。我们期待与读者们一起从河南故事中汲取更多的智慧和力量，共同创造更加美好的未来。

Series Foreword

China is one of the four ancient civilizations in the world, and is also the only country in the world where the ancient civilization has not been interrupted. Located in east-central China, Henan Province is an important cradle for the Chinese nation and Chinese civilization. In the course of the five thousand years of Chinese history, for more than three thousand years it served as the political, economic and cultural center of the country and therefore, as generally accepted, represents half of the history of China. Henan is the native place of Yellow Emperor, the cradle of Chinese culture, the starting point of the ancient Silk Road in the east, and the birthplace of Shaolin Kungfu and Chen-style Taijiquan—typical examples of the world-renowned Chinese martial arts. It was here that the earliest capital city in China was founded, the oldest Chinese characters engraved, and the earliest commerce took shape.

In the new era, Henan has witnessed rapid growth in its economy and remarkable improvement of people's living conditions owing to the national reform and opening-up policy and unremitting endeavors of the people. Modern economic achievements and social development as well as the changes of way of life could be traced back to its traditional values and cultural heritages. To enable people from other countries to understand Henan, and let the Province integrate more efficiently into the world development, the Foreign Affairs Office of the People's Government of Henan Province has organized teams of authoritative experts and scholars in relevant fields to compile this *Chinese Civilization: Stories from Henan* in Chinese and foreign languages since 2018 by crystallizing the excellence of traditions and outstanding features of modern development. The book series include *The Yellow River Culture, Heluo Culture, Laozi, Zhuangzi, The Yellow Emperor, Shaolin Kungfu, Taijiquan, Traditional Chinese Medicine,*

Chinese Characters, The Silk Road, Ancient Chinese Capitals, Feeding the People—Agriculture, The Grand Canal, Cultural Heritage, Ceramic, Bronze, Handicraft Art, Calligraphy, Acrobatics, Henan Cuisine, Henan Opera, Poverty Alleviation, Silk Road in the Air, Zhengzhou—An Aviation City, South-to-North Water Diversion, Grain of the Central Plains, Man-Made River—Hongqiqu Canal, A Model Official—Jiao Yulu, etc., presenting a panoramic picture of the Province.

In today's world, human civilization has made great progress in both material accumulation and ethical advancement, and the great abundance of materials today, especially, is beyond the imagination of the ancient people. At the same time, however, modern people are also confronted with a lot of problems, such as the widening gap between the rich and the poor, the indulgence in pursuit of luxury and extravagance, the undesirable extension of individualism, the decline of social integrity, and the increasingly tense relationship between man and nature. To solve the problems, we need to draw on the wisdom and powers developed today as well as those accumulated in the past. Henan is endowed with rich historical and cultural heritages characterized by its inclusiveness, and such heritages remain significant today. The intelligence and wisdom in Henan culture are conducive to self-cultivation and to the promotion of social development. The spirit of serving the people and relentless struggle, as embodied in Jiao Yulu and the man-made river—Hongqiqu Canal provides source of strength for building a community with a shared future for mankind. It is our hope that wisdom and strength from Henan stories could lead us to a shared brilliant future.

前　言

黄河是中华民族的母亲河，孕育了古老而伟大的中华文明，黄河流域的生态保护与高质量发展具有重大意义。习近平总书记于 2019 年 9 月 18 日在黄河流域生态保护和高质量发展座谈会上的讲话，进一步强调了实现黄河流域高质量发展的历史意义和伟大使命。

黄河流域在国民经济发展及人民生活过程起到重要的保障作用，以全国百分之二的河流径流量，承担着全国百分之十二人口、百分之十五耕地的用水需求。黄河流域为国家重要粮食基地，也是粮食安全的关键保障区，黄淮海平原主产区、汾渭平原主产区和河套灌区主产区三个粮食主产区的肉类及粮食产量已占全国的 1/3，体现了黄河流域在保障全国粮食产量及安全方面的重要地位。

黄河流域能源资源富集，流域的煤炭、石油、天然气和有色金属资源储量丰富，是我国重要的能源、化工、原材料和基础工业基地。在习近平生态文明思想的引领下，黄河流域产业发展逐步由以传统资源消耗为主的煤炭、钢铁、化工、石油、轻工纺织、机械制造等传统产业向以低碳、绿色为属性的新能源、新材料及绿色制造产业过渡，进一步凸显科技创新和战略性新兴产业的引领作用。

黄河流域孕育了河湟文化、关中文化、河洛文化、齐鲁文化等特色鲜明的地域文化，在黄河重大国家战略支撑下，黄河流域以传承黄河文化为起点，创新布局旅游业高质量发展，发挥黄河文化产业的品牌和示范引领作用，有效推动“旅游 +”融合发展过程。

以中心城市发展为引领，实现黄河流域城市群的高效建设和有序发展。充分发挥西安和郑州中心城市在黄河流域的辐射驱动作用，发挥其交通、资源、文化优势，充分推动周边城市的高质量发展。通过强化合作，推动以兰州和西宁为双中心的兰西城市群、以银川为中心的宁夏沿黄城市群、以呼和浩特为中心的呼包鄂榆城市群、以西安为中心的关中平原城市群、以太原为中心的晋中城市群、以郑州为中心的中原城市群、以济南和青岛为双中心的山东半岛城市群的高质量建设。

在黄河重大国家战略的持续引领下，黄河流域将持续发挥其资源、创新及粮食保障属性，推动中心城市及城市群建设及发展，使其真正成为造福人民的幸福河。

2023 年 7 月 28 日

《黄河流域高质量发展》编写组

Preface

The Yellow River is seen as the mother river of the Chinese nation, giving birth to the ancient and great Chinese civilization. The ecological protection and high-quality development of the Yellow River Basin are of great significance. General Secretary Xi Jinping's speech at the Symposium on Ecological Protection and High-Quality Development of the Yellow River Basin on 18 September 2019 further emphasized the historical significance and great mission of realizing the high-quality development of the Yellow River Basin.

This basin plays an important role in the development of the national economy and people's lives, with 2% of the country's river runoff, meeting the water demand of 12% of the country's population and 15% of arable land. In addition, the Yellow River Basin is an important national grain base and a key area for food security. The meat and grain output of the three major grain-producing areas—namely the Huang-Huai-Hai Plain, the Fen-Wei Plain, and the Hetao Irrigation Area—accounts for one-third of the country's total, reflecting the importance of the Yellow River Basin in ensuring national grain output and security.

The Yellow River Basin is furthermore rich in energy resources, such as coal, oil, natural gas, and non-ferrous metals, making it an important energy, chemical, raw material, and basic industrial base in China. Under the guidance of General Secretary Xi Jinping's idea of ecological civilization, the industrial development of the Yellow River Basin has gradually transitioned from traditional industries such as coal, iron and steel, chemical, petroleum, light textile, and machinery manufacturing, which mainly consume traditional resources, to the development of new energy sources, new materials and green manufacturing industries characterized by low-carbon emissions, further highlighting the leading role of scientific and technological innovation and strategic emerging industries.

The Yellow River Basin has also nurtured distinctive regional cultures such as Hehuang culture, Guanzhong culture, Heluo culture, and Qilu culture. Supported by the Major National Strategy of the Yellow River, the Yellow River Basin takes the inheritance of Yellow River culture as the starting point, aims to develop a modern layout of high-quality tourism development, plays the brand-and-demonstration leading role of the Yellow River cultural industry, and effectively promotes an integrated development of "Tourism plus".

With the development of central cities as the guide, the achievement of an efficient construction and orderly development of the Yellow River Basin city cluster is aimed for. The central cities of Xi 'an and Zhengzhou are meant to play a radiation-driven role in the Yellow River Basin and give play to their advantages in transportation, resources, and culture to fully promote a high-quality development of the surrounding cities. By strengthening cooperation, the purpose is to achieve a high-quality construction of the following urban regions: the Lanzhou-Xining city cluster with Lanzhou and Xining as its twin centers, the city cluster along the Yellow River in Ningxia with Yinchuan as its center, the Hohhot-Baotou-Ordos-Yulin city cluster with Hohhot as its center, the Guanzhong Plain city cluster with Xi'an as its center, the Jinzhong city cluster with Taiyuan as its center, the Central Plains city cluster with Zhengzhou as its center, and the Shandong Peninsula city cluster with Jinan and Qingdao as its twin centers.

Under the continuous guidance of the Major National Strategy of the Yellow River, the Yellow River Basin strives to constantly play its role in terms of resources, innovation, and grain security, promoting the construction and development of central cities and city clusters, turning the Yellow River truly into a river of happiness and comfort for the benefit of the people.

Editors and Authors of *High-quality Development of the Yellow River Basin*

July 28, 2023

目　录　　Contents

第一章

农业高质量发展与乡村振兴

Chapter 1

High-quality Development of Agriculture and Rural Revitalization

黄河流域具有重要的粮食生产及储量保障功能，在保障粮食生产的基础上，黄河流域正大力发展节水农业、绿色农业，实现农业的高质量发展。通过强化农村一二三产业发展融合，实现农村和农业发展的协同推进。

黄河流域农业生产总体产值大，呈现黄河下游河南、山东领先，上游四川体量大，其他省区产值略低的现状。这与各省区的自然条件、人口分布、基础资源等密切相关。

一、粮食生产与保障

黄河流域是国家重要粮食基地，也是我国粮食安全的关键保障区。在全国十三个粮食主产区中黄河流域占据了三个，黄淮海平原主产区、汾渭平原主产区和河套灌区主产区的肉类及粮食产量已占全国的1/3。在2022年全国粮食产量排行榜中，河南、山东、内蒙古分别占据第二、第三、第六的前列位置，充分体现了黄河流域在保障全国粮食产量及储量方面的重要地位。依托黄河流域在粮食生产和稳定保障方面的关键地位，国家也在大力推进黄河流域河南省等粮食主产区向粮食生产核心区的建设。

黄河流域各粮食主产区省份在保障国家粮食安全、提升粮食核心竞争力方面发挥了重要作用。其中，河南省粮食产量已顺利由1000亿斤跨越进入1300亿斤，实现了产量的稳定持续增长，农业农村部也在通

The Yellow River Basin fulfills the important functions of guaranteeing grain production and storage capacity. On the basis of guaranteeing grain production, the Yellow River Basin has been vigorously developing water-efficient agriculture as well as green agriculture to achieve high-quality development of agriculture. By integrating the development of primary, secondary, and tertiary industries in rural areas, a synergy of rural and agricultural development can be achieved.

The overall output value of agricultural production in the Yellow River Basin is high, with currently the output value of Henan and Shandong in the lower reaches of the Yellow River taking the lead, the output value of Sichuan in the upper reaches is high, and the output value of other provinces is slightly lower. This is closely correlated with natural conditions, population distribution, and basic resources of each province.

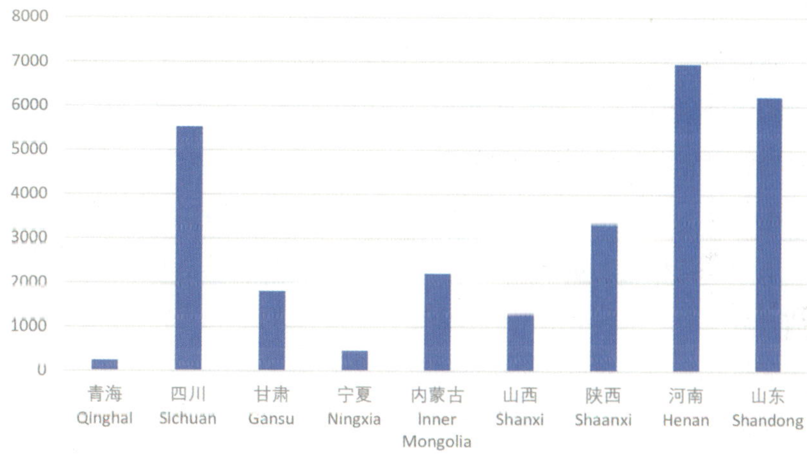

黄河流域各省份2022年农业总产值（亿元）

Gross Agricultural Output Value of Yellow River Basin Provinces in 2022 (Hundred million/Yuan)

I. Grain Production and Security

The Yellow River Basin is a nationally important grain base and a key area for grain security in China. The Yellow River Basin accounts for three of the country's thirteen major grain-producing areas. The meat and grain output of the major production areas of the Huang-Huai-Hai Plain, Fen-Wei Plain, and

过战略合作、政策支持等渠道强化推动河南省建设成为粮食生产核心区。山东、内蒙古等省区的粮食产量也分别进入 1100 亿斤、760 亿斤的行列，为黄河流域粮食生产提供有效保障。

黄河流域粮食作物主要以小麦、玉米及水稻为主。流域面积广阔，随上中下游地形及气候的变化，各省区的主要粮食品种也呈现一定差异。黄河上游的青海主要以小麦、青稞为主产粮食作物，宁夏以水稻、小麦、玉米为主，甘肃以小麦、玉米、马铃薯为主，内蒙古则主要以小麦、大豆、玉米、马铃薯为主。黄河中游的陕西和山西，则主要以玉米、小麦、豆类和薯类为主。下游的河南主要以水稻、小麦、玉米为主，而山东以小麦、玉米、薯类为主。

1. 黄淮海平原主产区

黄淮海平原是国内最大的平原区域，总面积约为 31 万平方千米。北起燕山山脉的南麓，南抵桐柏山、大别山北麓，西起太行山、秦岭东麓，东临渤海和黄海。其涉及的省份主要包括山东、河南、河北、江苏及安徽五省，也包含北京、天津两市。黄淮海平原主产区是中国粮食主产区之一，其粮食产量逐年攀升，对保障国家粮食安全具有重大意义。同时，黄淮海平原的耕地面积居全国各一级农区之首，进一步凸显了其在国家粮食储备方面的重大战略地位和意义。

对接黄河重大国家战略，黄淮海平原正逐步加快农业现代化发展，通过优质农产品研发和科技创新融入，打造优质专用小麦产业带、棉花产业带、大豆产业带和玉米产业带，并辐射带动畜牧业产业带的高效发展。

Hetao Irrigation Area, constitutes one third of the entire country's total. Henan, Shandong, and Inner Mongolia take second, third, and sixth places respectively in the national grain output ranking in 2022, fully reflecting the significant position of the Yellow River Basin in ensuring national grain output and reserves. Relying on the key position of the Yellow River Basin in the production and stable supply of grain, the country is also vigorously promoting Henan Province and other major grain-producing areas in the Yellow River Basin towards core grain production areas.

The major grain-producing provinces in the Yellow River Basin have played an important role in ensuring national grain security and improving the core competitiveness of grain. Among them, the grain output of Henan Province has successfully exceeded 50 million tons and even reached 65 million tons, achieving a steady and sustained growth in output. The Ministry of Agriculture and Rural Affairs is also strengthening the upgrade of Henan Province to the level of core area of grain production through strategic cooperation, policy support, and other means. The grain output of Shandong and Inner Mongolia has also reached 55 million tons and 38 million tons respectively, providing an effective guarantee for grain production in the Yellow River Basin.

Wheat, corn, and rice are the main grain crops in the Yellow River Basin. The basin covers a vast area, and varies with the topography and climate of the upper and lower reaches, and the main grain varieties of different provinces and regions also show certain differences. In the upper reaches of the Yellow River, mainly the following is harvested: Qinghai produces grain crops with wheat and highland barley; Ningxia primarily produces rice, wheat and corn; Gansu mostly grows wheat, corn and potatoes; Inner Mongolia mainly produces wheat, soybean, corn, and potatoes. In the middle reaches of the Yellow River, Shaanxi and Shanxi mainly grow and harvest corn, wheat, beans, and tubers. In the lower reaches of the Yellow River, Henan mainly produces rice, wheat, and corn, while Shandong mainly produces wheat, corn, and tubers.

1. The Major Production Area of the Huang-Huai-Hai Plain

The Huang-Huai-Hai Plain is the largest plain area in China, covering a total area of about 310,000 square kilometers. It extends from the southern foot of the Yanshan Mountains in the north, to the Tongbai Mountains and the

2. 汾渭平原主产区

汾渭平原是黄河中游最大的冲积平原，面积约为 7 万平方千米，为国内第四大平原，主要涉及省份为陕西、山西和河南，该区域历史悠久，承载着黄河中游诸多文化遗迹及资源。其粮食作物以强筋、中筋小麦为主。

积极对接黄河重大国家战略，汾渭平原与河套灌区建立高效对接机制，倡导实现创新资源及农业要素的高效分配，推广优质粮食品种的研发及种植，建立并推广高品质农田及相关标准，构建农业绿色循环生态产业链，正逐步形成粮食主产核心区。

3. 河套灌区粮食主产区

河套灌区是黄河流域中游灌区，处于黄河内蒙古段“几”字弯位置，总土面积达 1784 万亩，是设计灌溉面积最大的灌区，在黄河流域乃至全国保障粮食和农产品生产方面具有日益突出的意义。河套灌区正通过优质粮食品种种植及标准化农田建设，实现粮食主产区的农业现代化。

河套灌区已列入水利部评选的国家二十个示范灌区之一，也成功入选世界灌溉工程遗产名录，在世界范围产生了重要影响。

northern foot of the Dabie Mountains in the south, the Taihang Mountains and the eastern foothills of the Qinling Mountains in the west, and the Bohai Sea and the Yellow Sea in the east. The provinces involved here mainly include Shandong, Henan, Hebei, Jiangsu and Anhui, as well as Beijing and Tianjin. The major agricultural area of the Huang-Huai-Hai Plain is one of the primary grain-producing areas in China, and its grain yield has been rising year after year, which is of great significance in guaranteeing national food security. At the same time, the arable land area of the Huang-Huai-Hai Plain is the vastest among all primary agricultural regions in China, further highlighting its significant strategic position and value in terms of national grain reserves.

Adhering to the major national strategy of the Yellow River, the Huang-Huai-Hai Plain is gradually accelerating agricultural modernization. Through the research and development of high-quality agricultural products and the integration of scientific and technological innovation, the Huang-Huai-Hai Plain plans to create a high-quality special wheat industry belt, a cotton industry belt, a soybean industry belt, and a corn industry belt, and to radiate and drive its efficient development of the livestock industry belt.

2. The Main Production Area of the Fen-Wei Plain

The Fen-Wei Plain is the largest alluvial plain in the middle area of the Yellow River, covering a territory of about 70,000 square kilometers and is the fourth largest plain in China, largely pertaining to the provinces of Shaanxi, Shanxi, and Henan. The region has a long history and carries many cultural relics and resources in the middle reaches of the Yellow River. Its grain crops are mainly strong and medium gluten wheat.

Actively following the major national strategy of the Yellow River, the Fen-Wei Plain and Hetao Irrigation Area have established an efficient docking mechanism, support the efficient allocation of innovative resources and other agricultural factors, promote the research and development and cultivation of high-quality grain varieties, establish and promote the best farmland quality and related standards, build a green industrial chain for agriculture, and are gradually forming a major grain production area.

3. The Chief Food Production Area of the Hetao Irrigation Area

Located in the middle portions of the Yellow River Basin, the Hetao

二、节水农业

黄河流域属于典型的资源型缺水区域，且上、中、下游各省份水资源状况差异较大。黄河流域以全国百分之二的河流径流量，承担着全国百分之十二人口、百分之十五耕地的用水需求，水资源总体开发利用率较高。依托较匮乏的水资源量承担着沿岸九省区的粮食、农作物种植，也承担了黄淮海平原主产区、汾渭平原主产区和河套灌区主产区的农业生产和粮食产出。

黄河流域节水农业稳步推进发展

Steady Development of Water-Efficient Agriculture in the Yellow River Basin

在 2022 年，水资源一级区供水量中黄河区的农业用水量达 258.9 亿立方米，已占用水总量的 66.11%，充分表明黄河流域农业节水的潜能巨大。近年来，黄河流域节水农业发展在工程建设、规章制度及关键技术开发等方面有了长足进步。

Irrigation Area is situated at the "几" (Ji, a Chinese character)-shaped bend of the Inner Mongolia section of the Yellow River, with a total land area of 17.84 million *mu* (about 11,893.39 square kilometers). This makes it the largest irrigation district in terms of a specially designed irrigation area and therefore of increasing significance in safeguarding food and agricultural production in the Yellow River Basin and the country as a whole. In addition, the Hetao Irrigation Area is modernizing agriculture in their principal grain-growing fields through the cultivation of high-quality grain varieties and the construction of standardized farmland.

The Hetao Irrigation Area has been listed as one of the 20 national demonstration irrigation areas selected by the Ministry of Water Resources and has also been successfully listed in the World Heritage List of Irrigation Projects, which has exerted great influence worldwide.

II. Water-Efficient Agriculture

The Yellow River Basin is a typical water-scarce region in terms of resources, and the water resources of the upper, middle, and lower reaches vary greatly. The Yellow River Basin supports the water consumption of 12% of the country's population and 15% of the arable land with 2% of the country's river runoff, which means the overall development and utilization rate of water resources in the Yellow River Basin is quite high. Relying on relatively scarce water resources, the Yellow River nevertheless supports the cultivation of food and crops in the nine provinces and regions along its banks, and it also meets the water needs of agriculture and grain production in the principal areas of the Huang-Huai-Hai Plain, Fen-Wei Plain, and Hetao Irrigation Area.

In the year 2022, the agricultural water consumption in the Yellow River area of the first-class water resource zone, amounted to 25.89 billion cubic meters, which already accounts for 66.11% of the total water consumption, fully demonstrating the huge potential for agricultural water conservation in the Yellow River Basin. In recent years, the development of water-efficient agriculture in the Yellow River Basin has made considerable progress in terms of engineering

1. 农业节水工程建设

黄河流域正逐步大力推动上游甘肃黄河高抽灌区 / 宁蒙引黄灌区、中游汾渭灌区、下游引黄灌区等关键灌区的配套建设及实质升级改造过程。在 2019 年，黄河流域农田灌溉水有效利用系数达 0.562，节水水平总体优于全国水平。在《水利部关于实施黄河流域深度节水控水行动的意见》指引下，沿黄各省份也相继推出引黄灌区农业节水工程建设方案等具体措施，旨在 2025 年前达成农业灌溉用水有效利用系数进一步提升至 0.586 的目标。

2. 完善节水制度制定与落实

流域水资源量较为有限，节水潜力存在但受到明显制约。黄河流域正逐步强化农业水资源的需求和供给管理，深度节水行动也正逐步实施。黄河重大国家战略提出以来，正在制定流域整体和各省份的节水制度及相关保障落实措施，如《水利部关于实施黄河流域深度节水控水行动的意见》等，推动实施以水资源动态监测为控制手段的流域节水管控体系。

3. 节水关键技术研发

依托黄河流域各科研机构及科技力量，正大力研发基于灌溉节水成套机械装备、新产品及技术方案，取得了一系列的关键设备及配套工艺的高效集成。位于黄河流域下游的河南新乡市的中国农业科学院农田灌溉研究所也在强化推动节水关键技术及设备研发方面作出重要贡献。

4. 节水促进乡村振兴

宁夏贺兰县地处宁夏北部引黄灌区核心地带，近年来通过引入“一水多用、一田多产”的节水模式，实现农业用水在“稻田 - 环沟 - 鱼池”各子部分的闭合循环，最大限度地实现了水的高效率使用。相较于传统灌溉及用水模式，贺兰县的稻渔种养模式可实现节水 30% 以上，化肥用量减少 40% 以上，同时大大降低了农药的使用量。该节水模式的使用，不仅未降低农产品的质量，反而有效提升了稻米产品的品质，特色

construction, regulatory framework, and key technology development.

1. Construction of Water-Efficient Projects in Agriculture

The Yellow River Basin has been gradually and vigorously constructing needed infrastructure and substantially upgrading key irrigation areas such as the upstream Gansu Yellow River High-pressure Pumping Irrigation Area, the Ningxia-Inner Mongolia Yellow River Irrigation Area, the midstream Fen-Wei Irrigation Area, and the downstream Yellow River Irrigation Area. In 2019, the effective utilization coefficient of agricultural irrigation water in the Yellow River Basin reached 0.562, and the overall level of water conservation bested the national level. Under the guidance of the "Opinions of the Ministry of Water Resources on Implementing In-depth Water Saving and Water Controlling in the Yellow River Basin", the provinces around the Yellow River also have launched specific projects such as the construction program of agricultural water conservation projects in the Yellow River irrigation district, aiming to increase the effective utilization coefficient of agricultural irrigation water to 0.586 by 2025.

2. To Better Develop an Agricultural Water Efficiency System

With limited freshwater resources, the basin has a water efficiency potential which is obviously restricted. The government has gradually been strengthening the demand and supply management of agricultural water resources in the Yellow River Basin. In addition, in-depth water-efficient action is gradually implemented. Since the major national strategy of the Yellow River was put forward, the water-efficient system and relevant guarantee measures for the whole basin and each province have been formulated, such as the "Opinions of the Ministry of Water Resources on Implementing In-depth Water Saving and Water Controlling in the Yellow River Basin", etc., to promote the water-efficient management and control system through the dynamic monitoring of water resources in the basin.

3. Research and Development of Key Agricultural Water-Efficient Technologies

Relying on various research institutions and scientific and technological forces in the Yellow River Basin, we are energetically developing complete sets of machinery equipment, new products, and technical solutions based on water-efficient irrigation, and have been able to achieve a series of efficient integration of key equipment and matching processes. The Institute of Farmland Irrigation of

中国农业科学院农田灌溉研究所试验田

Experimental Field of Institute of Farmland Irrigation of CAAS

品牌产品的稻米不断推向市场，提升了居民收入。同时，良好的稻渔产业布局也进一步提升了区域的观光旅游功能，形成了特色的稻田景色，不断吸引游客的到来，大大促进了乡村旅游业发展。

位于黄河“几”字弯最顶端的鄂尔多斯市达拉特旗属于以农业为主的区域，长期受制于水资源利用率低的负面影响。近年来，达拉特旗引入节水灌溉与智慧农业技术，逐步推动高标准农田的建设工作，打造了万亩高标准农田示范区，将水、肥等精准地输送到农田作物的根部，大大减少了水肥的过程损失，亩均种植成本降低 180－220 元，减少农民的种植成本，有效提升了收入。

the Chinese Academy of Agricultural Sciences in Xinxiang City, Henan Province, located in the lower portions of the Yellow River Basin, is also making important contributions to strengthening the promotion of water-efficient key technologies and equipment research and development.

4. Water-saving Promotes Rural Revitalization

Helan County in Ningxia Hui Autonomous Region is located in the core area of the Yellow River irrigation district in northern Ningxia. In recent years, by introducing a water-saving model of "one water for multiple uses, one field for multiple yields", Helan County has achieved a closed-loop cycle of agricultural water use in the "paddy field, ditch, fish pond" system, maximizing the efficient use of water. Compared to traditional irrigation and water use patterns, Helan County's rice and fish farming model can achieve over 30% water saving and reduce fertilizer usage by over 40%, while significantly reducing the amount of pesticides used. The use of this water-saving model not only does not compromise the quality of agricultural products, but effectively enhances the quality of rice products. Rice products under unique brand names have been continuously

湟水河湿地公园

The Huangshuihe River Wetland Park

三、绿色农业

绿色农业的核心是绿色农田建设和农业高质量发展，坚持生态优先和绿色发展的理念，实现流域农业生产要素及创新资源的高效配置，强化农业生产的过程管理和优化控制，以实现生产过程及终端产品的绿色化、标准化。

1. 湟水河等水源地区域有机农业发展

湟水河是黄河的重要支流，承担着给流域居民提供饮用水的重要功能。依托水源地的关键功能和属性要求，湟水河所在区域的农业发展依托生态文明建设展开，强化有机农业的发展，如湟源县正打造高品质农畜牧业品牌及相关产业，实现环境保护与农业发展的有机结合。

2. 洮河有机绿色农业发展

洮河

Taohe River

洮河是位于黄河南岸的重要支流，年水量仅次于渭河。其发源于青海省，一路流入甘肃省，并在甘肃省永靖县刘家峡库区实现汇入黄河。

introduced to the market, increasing residents' income. At the same time, the well-planned rice and fish farming industry has further enhanced the region' s tourism function, forming distinctive rice field landscapes and attracting tourists, greatly promoting the development of rural tourism.

Dalad Banner, located at the top end of the "几"-shaped curve of the Yellow River, is mainly an agricultural region that has long been negatively affected by low water resource utilization. In recent years, Dalad Banner has introduced water-saving irrigation and smart agriculture technologies, gradually promoting the construction of high-standard farmland and creating a demonstration area of tens of thousands of acres of high-standard farmland. Water and fertilizer are precisely delivered to the roots of crops, greatly reducing water and fertilizer losses in the process. The per-acre planting cost has been reduced by about 180-220 yuan, reducing farmers' planting costs and effectively increasing their income.

Ⅲ.Sustainable Agriculture

The essence of green agriculture is the construction of green farmland and high-quality agricultural development, adhering to the concept of ecological priority and green development, realizing an efficient allocation of agricultural means of production and innovative resources in the basin, and strengthening process management and optimal control of industrial farming in order to achieve green and standardized production processes and end products.

1. Regional Organic Agricultural Development of the Huangshuihe River and Other Water Source Areas

The Huangshuihe River is a major tributary of the Yellow River, which fulfills the critical function of providing drinking water to the residents of the basin. Relying on the key functions and attribute requirements of water sources, the agricultural development of the Huangshuihe River Basin is based on the idea of building an ecological civilization and strengthening the development of organic agriculture. For example, Huangyuan County is developing high-end brands of agriculture and livestock as well as related industries, for the purpose of realizing an organic combination of environmental protection and agricultural development.

洮河国家级自然保护区具有原始的生态系统，以保护为核心的绿色农业发展模式在逐步推广，以草田轮作、轮作休耕为主要耕种方式，以最大程度保护农田及自然生态环境。

3. 黄河流域农业示范区建设及农业绿色发展

近年来，杨凌农业高新技术产业示范区和黄河三角洲大力推动绿色农业发展。杨凌农业高新技术产业示范区以农业创新技术的研究和应用为核心，致力于农业创新产品及设备的研发过程，每年在此举办的农业高新博览会成为重要的宣传和交流平台。

黄河三角洲受制于黄河中上游来水的影响，存在因中上游水量减小导致的断流及水资源匮乏现象。其推动“以水定产”，在充分、合理利用黄河来水基础上，充分挖掘陆域与海域的协同延伸潜力，构建基于现代生态工程技术与高效农业设备的绿色生态农业模式，加强黄河三角洲农业高新技术产业示范区的建设。

杨凌示范区

Yangling Demonstration Zone

2. Organic Green Agricultural Development of the Taohe River

The Taohe River also is a major tributary on the south bank of the Yellow River, with an annual water volume second only to the Weihe River. It originates in Qinghai Province, flows into Gansu Province, and merges into the Yellow River at the Liujiaxia reservoir area in Yongjing County, Gansu Province. The Taohe River National Nature Reserve is an original ecosystem and is gradually adopting a green agricultural development model with sustainability as its core, with grass and crop rotation as well as land fallow as the main farming methods, in an attempt to protect farmland and the natural ecological environment to the greatest extent.

3. Agricultural Demonstration Zone Construction and Green Agricultural Development of the Yellow River Basin

In recent years, the Yangling Agricultural High-Tech Industry Demonstration Zone and the Yellow River Delta have industriously promoted the development of green agriculture. Focusing on the research and application of agricultural innovative technology, the Yangling Agricultural High-Tech Industry Demonstration Zone has been devoting itself to the research and development process of agricultural innovative products and equipment, and the annual China Yangling Agricultural High-Tech Fair has become an important platform for publicity and networking.

The Yellow River Delta is subject to the incoming water in the upper and middle reaches of the Yellow River, and there is a phenomenon of water flow cut-off and water shortage caused by the decrease of water volume in the upper and middle parts. The Yellow River Delta promotes "determining production according to available water resources". On the basis of fully and properly utilizing the incoming water carried by the Yellow River, it fully taps into the synergistic extension potential of land and sea areas, attempts to build a green ecological agriculture mode based on modern ecological engineering technology and efficient farming equipment, and strengthens the construction of agricultural high-tech industry demonstration zones in the Yellow River Delta.

4. Green Agriculture Promotes Rural Revitalization

Jishishan County in Gansu, located near the upstream water conservation area of the Yellow River, focuses on ecological restoration and has developed green

黄河三角洲湿地

Yellow River Delta Wetland

agriculture through various channels, such as establishing sightseeing agricultural demonstration parks, cultivating distinctive crops, and implementing eco-friendly projects. The county has cultivated 149,500 *mu* (9967 hectares) of specialty crops and gradually promoted the development of a characteristic cultural and tourism industry based on green agriculture.

Based on its environmental conditions, Gaoqing County in Shandong has developed green and distinctive agriculture to support rural revitalization. Leveraging advantages such as sandy soil, significant temperature differences between day and night, and convenient irrigation from the Yellow River, Gaoqing County has formed a brand effect in its specialty agricultural products industry, building upon effective ecological restoration efforts. With the irrigation of the Yellow River water, over ten agricultural products, including Gaoqing rice, Gaoqing watermelons, and Gaoqing tomatoes, have been granted Chinese geographical indication trademarks and are widely welcomed in the market. This has effectively boosted the income and quality of life for residents along the riverbank.

IV. Integrated Development of Primary, Secondary, and Tertiary Industries in Rural Areas

Based on the important strategic position and value of the agricultural industry in the Yellow River Basin, modern operation modes (such as industrial chain and value chain) should be efficiently integrated into agricultural and rural developments, so as to realize an organic integration of agricultural production, multi-level agricultural products processing, multi-channel sales, multi-functional expansion and the supporting service industry in the upper, middle and lower reaches of the Yellow River Basin, and the promotion of an integrated development of primary, secondary, and tertiary industries in rural areas of the Yellow River Basin.

Qinghai Province vigorously promotes the transformation into a green and organic agricultural and livestock products demonstration province. As a

4. 绿色农业促进乡村振兴

位于黄河上游水源涵养地附近的甘肃积石山县在注重生态修复的基础上，通过建立观光农业示范园、种植特色农作物、增设生态环保项目等多种渠道发展绿色农业，形成特色农作物 14.95 万亩，并逐步推动建设基于绿色农业的特色文旅产业。

山东省高青县基于自身环境禀赋条件，发展绿色特色农业，支撑乡村振兴。有效依托其沙质土壤条件、昼夜温差大、黄河灌溉便利等优势条件，在前期有效生态修复的基础上，发展形成了具有品牌效应的特色农产品产业。在黄河水灌溉下，高青大米、高青西瓜、高青西红柿等十余种中国地理标志商标认定的农产品，在市场上受到广泛的欢迎，有效提升了沿岸居民的收入和幸福生活水平。

四、农村一二三产业发展融合

基于农业产业在黄河流域的重要战略地位和价值，将产业链和价值链等现代化的运营方式高效融入农业及农村发展，实现黄河流域上中下游区域农业生产、不同层次农产品加工、多渠道销售、多功能拓展、配套服务业有机融合等，促进黄河流域农村一二三产业融合发展。

青海省大力推动绿色有机农畜产品示范省建设。作为黄河流域上游的高海拔省份，青海省以其独特的高原资源禀赋，正着力推动基于绿色有机农畜产品发展示范省建设，并基于生态旅游资源，形成天然旅游服务业与绿色有机畜牧业融合的产业发展模式，以高新技术与数字经济融入农业一二三产业的高效发展。

四川省培育特色农业、实现产品产出与品牌发展的融合。在黄河上游，四川省以其特色农业发展著称，正在建设当地特色的现代农业发展体系，逐步培育发展特色农业及产品，挖掘更为持续的一二三产业融合连锁机制。以彭山区果园村（万亩葡萄园）、“公司＋基地＋蔬菜专业

high-altitude province in the upper reaches of the Yellow River Basin, Qinghai Province (with its unique plateau resource endowment) is making great efforts to become a demonstration province based on the development of green and organic agricultural and livestock products. And based on eco-tourism resources, it has adopted an industrial development mode integrating the natural tourism service industry with green and organic livestock and integrating high-tech and digital economy into the efficient development of primary, secondary, and tertiary industries of agriculture.

Sichuan Province has been cultivating its characteristic agriculture and realizing the integration of product output and brand development. In the upper portions of the Yellow River, Sichuan Province is famous for its development of distinctive agriculture. It is building a modern agricultural development system with local traits, gradually cultivating and developing characteristic agriculture and products, and exploring a more sustainable chain mechanism for the integration of primary, secondary, and tertiary industries. The integrated development mode of primary, secondary, and tertiary industries—represented by Guoyuan Village in Pengshan District (10,000 *mu* vineyard or 667-hectare vineyard), the characteristic Sichuan pickle production mode of "company + base + vegetable professional cooperative", and the 10,000 *mu* (or 667 hectares) lemon plantation in Yuexian County — has become prominent.

Gansu Province builds an integrated development system of rural industries and strengthens the promotion of farming culture projects. Gansu Province is making every effort to stimulate the in-depth integration of agriculture and rural areas with cultural tourism, health and elderly care, and other industries. It reinforces the integrated development of agriculture by implementing the live transmission project of agricultural food culture, developing modern agriculture based on the Internet and big data, building close interest relationships between terminal enterprises, agri-businesses, and rural areas, and strengthening the joint-stock cooperation of agricultural production processes and products.

Ningxia promotes the construction of a demonstration park for the integration of primary, secondary, and tertiary industries in bio-agriculture, and advances a green and efficient development of agriculture. Based on Ningxia's ecological environment constraints and a resource superiority of characteristic

合作社”的特色四川泡菜生产模式及岳县万亩柠檬种植园等为代表的一二三产业融合发展模式凸显。

甘肃打造农村产业融合发展体系，强化推动农耕文化工程。甘肃省正全力推进农业农村与文化旅游、健康养老等产业的深度融合发展，通过实施农耕食文化活态传承项目、基于互联网/大数据为载体的现代农业发展、构建终端企业与农业农村的紧密利益联系、强化农业生产过程及产品的股份合作等，进一步强化农业的融合发展。

宁夏推动生物农业循一二三产业融合示范园建设，促进农业绿色高效发展。基于宁夏生态环境约束及特色农果产品资源优势，宁夏在构建以“微生物+”农业循环为核心的农村农业发展示范模式，构建集高端特色农产品开发、农业高新技术研发、农业废弃物高效循环利用为一体的农业农村生产、运营及提升新模式。宁夏国家葡萄及葡萄酒产业开放发展综合试验区也是国家首个特色产业开放发展综合试验区，对于推动农业一二三产业融合发展及高端农产品产出具有重要的引领示范作用。

内蒙古推动农牧业供给侧结构性改革，拓宽农牧业融合发展。以习近平生态文明思想为引领，内蒙古正以工业发展理念为依托，深入挖掘农牧业发展市场需求和农牧业终端产品牵引，突破农牧业传统发展过程中“一畜独大”“一粮独大”的薄弱单一结构，尝试和推动“粮改饲”

agricultural and fruit products, Ningxia is implementing a rural agricultural development demonstration model with a "microbial plus" agricultural cycle at its core, and establishing a new model of rural agricultural production, operation, and upgrading that integrates the development of high-end characteristic agricultural products, agricultural high-tech research and development, and efficient recycling of agricultural waste. The Ningxia National Comprehensive Pilot Zone for the Opening and Development of the Grape and Wine Industry is also the country's first comprehensive pilot area for the beginning and development of typical industries, which plays an important leading and exemplary role in promoting an integrated development of the primary, secondary, and tertiary industries of agriculture and the output of high-end agricultural products.

Inner Mongolia promotes supply-side structural reform of agriculture and animal husbandry and expands integrated development of agriculture and animal husbandry. Guided by Xi Jinping's idea of an ecological civilization and relying on the concept of industrial development, Inner Mongolia is further exploring market demand for agricultural and livestock development and the traction of agricultural and livestock end products, breaking through the weak and single structure of "one type of livestock alone" and "one kind of grain alone" in the traditional development process of agriculture and livestock, as well as working to promote the development ideas of "replacing grain with feeding" and "stabilizing sheep, increasing cattle, and expanding pigs and poultry".

Shaanxi accelerates the restructuring of its agricultural industry, and energetically promotes intensive processing of agricultural products. Shaanxi Province strengthens the promotion and planting of high-quality forage, achieves a coordinated development and promotion of a composite planting structure of grain, cash crops, and forage, vigorously refines a layout and output of its unique agricultural products such as kiwi fruit at the northern foot of the Qinling Mountains and Qinba shallow mountains, Weibei apples, red dates in the loess and bedrock area along the Yellow River, selenium-enriched organic food in southern Shaanxi Weibei, and minor grains in northern Shaanxi, as well as boosts the development of regional characteristic industries.

Shanxi implements the "Seven Clear", refining its land use requirements for the development of primary, secondary, and tertiary agricultural industries. Shanxi

和“稳羊增牛扩猪禽”发展思路。

陕西加快农业产业结构调整，大力推动农产品精深加工。陕西省加大优质饲草料的推广和种植，实现粮食、经济作物和饲草料复合种植结构的协调发展和推进工作，大力精深发展秦岭北麓及秦巴浅山区猕猴桃、渭北苹果、黄河沿岸土石山区红枣、陕南渭北富硒有机食品、陕北小杂粮的特色农产品的布局和产出，深化发展区域特色产业。

山西实施“七个明确”，细化农业一二三产业发展用地要求。山西省出台和实施《山西省保障和规范农村一二三产业融合发展用地实施细则》，以“七个明确”加以概括，在村庄建设边界外用地政策支持、农村土地综合整治权限、新增建设用地匹配指标、农村农业发展配套公共设施等方面予以了具体要求。近年来，山西大力推动农产品深加工及配套运输、服务管理等措施，取得了较大的进步。

河南省大力发展种业，建立优势特色农产品基地。河南省谋划设立种类基金，做大、做强种业公司，基于河南省的交通运输及物流优势，构建形成有辐射影响力的种业业态模式。逐步打造黄淮海平原粮食安全产业带河南核心片区，加快中国（驻马店）国际农产品加工产业园和周口国家农业高新技术产业示范区的建设工作，在巩义、孟津、宝丰、长垣、新县推动农村宅基地制度改革试点工作。

山东省构建优势特色产业集群、现代农业产业园区。目前，山东省已构建省级以上优势特色产业集群、现代农业产业园区达500多个，现代农业高效转型发展居所有产业新旧动能转换之首。积极发挥科技创新、产品研发及构建高端农产品在农业一二三产业融合方面的重大推动作用，构建形成重体验、重终端的高效产业链模式。

Province issued and implemented the "Implementation Rules of Shanxi Province for Guaranteeing and Regulating Land Use for the Integrated Development of Primary, Secondary, and Tertiary Industries in Rural Areas", which is summarized in the "Seven Clear". It generates specific requirements in terms of policy support for land use outside the village construction boundary, further provides authority for comprehensive improvement of rural land, matching indicators of new construction land, and supports public facilities for rural agricultural development and other aspects. In recent years, Shanxi has strongly promoted measures such as deep processing of agricultural products, supporting transportation, and service management, and it has made remarkable progress.

Henan Province energetically develops the seed industry and establishes a superior and characteristic agricultural product base. Henan plans to set up a variety fund to expand and bolster seed industry companies. Based on the transportation and logistics advantages of Henan, a seed industry business model with a wide influence will be developed and formed. Henan Province is gradually building the Henan core area of the grain security industrial belt in the Huang-Huai-Hai Plain, accelerating the construction of the China (Zhumadian) International Agricultural Product Processing Industrial Park and Zhoukou National Agricultural High-tech Industrial Demonstration Zone, and is promoting the pilot reform of the rural homestead system in the Gongyi, Mengjin, Baofeng, Changyuan, and Xinxian counties.

Shandong Province develops especially supported-characteristic industrial clusters and modern agricultural industrial parks. At present, Shandong Province has established more than 500 especially supported-typical industrial clusters above the regular provincial level together with modern agricultural industrial parks. The effective transformation and development of modern agriculture rank first among all industries in the conversion of both new and old kinetic energy sources. Shandong actively plays an important role in promoting scientific and technological innovation, product research and development, and the creation of top-level agricultural products through the integration of primary, secondary, and tertiary industries of agriculture; Shandong additionally develops and forms an efficient industrial chain model that focuses on experience and terminals.

五、推动乡村振兴

在党和国家政策的支持下，黄河流域大力推进乡村振兴战略，通过多种渠道的滩区移民、配套产业发展，构建乡村振兴产业链，实现黄河滩区安澜及经济大发展。通过积极挖掘黄河乡村旅游及文化资源，形成了基于黄河自然风貌的乡村旅游文化产业及红色旅游特色品牌。

1. 黄河乡村旅游及文化资源挖掘

阿河滩村为黄河上游青海省的第一个地质文化村，亦是黄河流域第一个以少数民族文化为属性的村落。阿河滩村所在的化隆县甘都镇以黄河生态保护和流域治理为契机，深入开展了流域治理的各项工作，有效改善了村落文化外貌和宜居环境。阿河滩村打造了系列的文化旅游、观光项目，形成了集旅游、生态、休闲、观光为一体的阿河滩村文化旅游示范地。

阿河滩地质文化村（央广网发 汪晓青摄）

Ahetan Geological Culture Village (Published by CNR News and photographed by Wang Xiaoqing)

V. Promotion of Rural Revitalization

With the support of the Party and national policies, the Yellow River Basin has industriously promoted a rural revitalization strategy. Through various channels of floodplain immigration and supporting industrial development, a rural revitalization industry chain has been constructed, achieving stability and economic development for the Yellow River floodplain. A rural tourism cultural industry and a red tourism characteristic brand, based on the natural features of the Yellow River, have been formed via active exploration of Yellow River rural tourism and cultural resources.

1. Yellow River Rural Tourism and Cultural Resources Excavation

Ahetan Village is the first geological culture village in Qinghai Province in the upper reaches of the Yellow River, and the first village in the basin with ethnic minority culture as its attribute. Gandu Town, Hualong County, where Ahetan Village is located, has taken the Yellow River ecological protection and basin governance as an opportunity to further carry out additional basin governance tasks, effectively enhancing the cultural appearance and livable environment of the village. Ahetan Village has since created a series of cultural tourism and sightseeing destinations, forming a cultural tourism demonstration site in the village that integrates tourism, ecology, leisure, and sightseeing.

As one of the twelve key red tourist attractions in China, the Shaanxi-Gansu-Ningxia old revolutionary base area in the middle reaches of the Yellow River was a key foothold of the Party Central Committee and the Workers' and Peasants' Red Army in the days of the Long March, representing significant historical and revolutionary value. However, due to the long-term influence of economic development and regional position, the development of red tourism resources and regional rural revitalization in the old revolutionary base area has been significantly limited. Since the 18th National Congress of the CPC, China has adopted a series of policies to support the development of tourism resources in the Shaanxi-Gansu-Ningxia old revolutionary base area and created the red tourism characteristic brand, and further exploited, used, and publicized the tourism resources in the old revolutionary base area with scientific and technological innovation. Based on Yan'an and Qingyang—two representative cities with red

黄河中游的陕甘宁革命老区作为全国重点红色旅游景区之一，是当时党中央和工农红军长征的关键落脚点，具有重要的历史和革命价值。但长期受制于经济发展和区域位置的影响，陕甘宁革命老区的红色旅游资源开发及区域乡村振兴受到了较大程度的限制。十八大以来，国家出台一系列政策助力陕甘宁革命老区的旅游资源开发、打造红色旅游特色品牌，以科技创新助力革命老区旅游资源的进一步挖掘和宣传。在延安和庆阳两个代表性红色旅游资源城市基础上，进一步在革命老区推动新农村建设和公共服务搭建过程，形成红色旅游资源发展与乡村振兴的协同推动机制。

延安革命纪念馆

Yan'an Revolutionary Memorial Hall

位于黄河下游的沂蒙革命老区在抗日战争、解放战争胜利及中华人

tourism resources—we will continue to encourage the construction of new rural areas and public services in the old revolutionary base area, in order to form a collaborative promotion mechanism for the development of red vacationing resources and rural revitalization.

The Yimeng old revolutionary base area, located downstream the Yellow River, played a crucial role in achieving victory during the War of Resistance Against Japanese Aggression, the Liberation War, and the founding of the People's Republic of China. Meanwhile, constrained by geographical and policy limitations, the economic and rural development of the Yimeng old revolutionary base area remains relatively backward. In the context of relevant national policies and following the Yellow River major national strategy, the Yimeng old revolutionary base area, thanks to measures such as modern logistics and live e-commerce, is progressively establishing an influential domestic live e-commerce base and hub. It relies on artificial intelligence, a developed logistics network, and logistics network support, and successfully transports deep-processed agricultural products (such as branded vegetables and honeysuckle) to the Yangtze River Delta and other places through more than 2,000 routes created, forming a production and sales platform of deep-processed agricultural products with brand recognition.

2. Migration Around the Yellow River and Supporting Industrial Development

Great rural development is achieved through an agricultural industrial chain of the Shala Village migration area. As a representative of this migration project in the reservoir region of Longyangxia Hydropower Station near the headwaters of the Yellow River, Shala Village, located in Mangqu Town, Guinan County, Qinghai Province boasts abundant land resources and complete infrastructural facilities. In the early stages of the migration and in the industrial development after the migration, Shala Village, financially supported by migration support funds and such departments as the water department, established a planting support base covering storage, screening, and processing as a whole and was accordingly equipped with agricultural machinery and other related hardware for every process. During the base development, its radiation effect gradually led to an integrated make-to-order industrial chain that currently includes base product

民共和国成立的过程中起到了关键推动作用。同样受制于地域及政策局限问题，沂蒙革命老区的经济发展及乡村建设相对落后。在国家相关政策及对接黄河重大国家战略背景下，沂蒙革命老区基于现代物流及电商直播等措施，正逐步打造形成国内有影响力的直播电商基地及枢纽，依托人工智能、发达物流网和物流网支撑，成功将精深加工农产品（如品牌蔬菜、金银花等）经打造的2000多条路线运输至长三角等地，形成了具有品牌影响力的精深加工农产品生产、销售基地。

沂蒙革命纪念馆
Yimeng Revolutionary Memorial Museum

2. 黄河移民及配套产业发展

沙拉村移民区域农业产业链实现农村大发展。作为黄河上游龙羊峡水电站库区移民工程的典型村，青海省贵南县茫曲镇沙拉村土地资源较为丰富、基础配套设施也较完善。在前期移民及移民后产业发展过程中，沙拉村依托移民扶持基金及水利部门等相关部门的资金支持，统筹建立了一个集仓储、筛分和加工等为一体的种植业扶持基地，并相应配

planting, deep processing, and transportation. In March 2022, Shala Village was elected as the representative of late-stage support for migration from large and medium-sized reservoirs nationwide, which is of great significance guiding the industrial development and poverty alleviation of reservoir immigration areas in the whole country.

Minning model village of Ningxia goes forward with the Minning Town that goes viral as a recent TV series. As a representative jointly-built immigration village in the western and eastern areas of China, Minning Village is located in the southwestern area of Yinchuan, a site designated by Xi Jinping already in 1997, and in later rural development, (based on the scientific planning and reasonable deployment of leaders) the relocated residents effectively ended poverty and achieved prosperity by developing characteristic industrial parks such as a grape park, a rural ecotourism park combing rice and fish farming, and promoting the Juncao technology industry through land transfer employing the technologies, talents, and concepts of the eastern region. By doing so, the Minning Village model came into being and has been applied to other areas effectively, thus forging a new model of poverty alleviation and prosperity in the eastern and western regions across the country, and it is of great reference significance.

The high-quality forestry and grass industry should be developed in the midstream beach areas of the Yellow River after the residents moved out. With vast and relatively flat lands, the southern beach areas of the midstream of the Yellow River allow for large-scale mechanized sowing, management, and harvesting, and can effectively combat soil erosion and dust by planting perennial forage grasses such as alfalfa. Henan Province is planning to promote the extensive planting of forage grasses in the original lands of the residents of beach areas through some key areas such as Zhongmu County, Xiangfu District of Kaifeng City, Lankao County, Yuanyang County, Fengqiu County, Changyuan City, Puyang County, Fan County, and Taiqian County, effectively integrating science and technology innovation and developing the southern beach areas of the river into a demonstration base of large-scale high-quality forage planting and innovative technology research and development.

Lijin County, at the estuary of the lower reaches of the Yellow River, implements the transformation and upgrading project of old village platforms,

贵南县沙拉村（图来自新华网）

Shala Village, Guinan County (From Xinhua News Network)

宁夏闽宁脱贫攻坚共同富裕示范区
Minning Demonstration Area of Poverty Alleviation and Common Prosperity, Ningxia

which can enhance the happiness of its residents. To effectively achieve flood prevention and tranquility of beach areas, most regions choose to relocate to ensure the safety of people's lives and property. However, some of them opt for in-situ reconstruction and modernization in the original place of residence due to the greater difficulty of relocation and the deep emotions invested in hometowns. For example, Lijin County at the mouth of the Yellow River has implemented the transformation and upgrading project of the old village platforms, which meets the basic requirements for the serenity of the downstream beach areas through elevating the ground level of residences and improving drainage projects. At the same time, it has established an agricultural development base integrating tourism, cultural heritage, elderly care, and leisure through overall planning and industrial integration development. At present, Lijin County has successfully built

套各过程的农机设备及相关机械设备。在扶持基地发展过程中，基于其辐射影响效应，逐步形成了“订单式”的基地产品种植、深加工及运输一体化产业链。2022 年 3 月，沙拉村移民区评选为全国大中型水库移民后期扶持典型案例，对于全国范围水库移民区域的产业发展及实现脱贫具有重要的指导意义。

打造宁夏闽宁示范村，携手“山海情”。闽宁村是典型的东西部共建移民村，1997 年由习近平亲自圈定银川西南玉泉营一带作为移民村的选址，在此后的乡村发展过程中，通过领导人的科学谋划和合理布局，基于东部地区的技术、人才、理念，通过土地流转发展葡萄等特色农业产业园、建设稻渔空间乡村生态观光园、推广菌草科技产业等有效实现了流域居民的脱贫致富，打造了闽宁示范村模式，并得以有效推广，在全国范围形成了东西部区域携手脱贫致富的新模式，并具有重要的借鉴价值。

黄河中游滩区利用原迁地大力发展优质林草业。黄河中游的河南滩区地域面积广袤、地势也较为平坦，适宜进行大面积的机械化播种、管理及收割操作，通过种植多年生的饲草如紫花苜蓿等，可有效抵抗水土流失及扬尘等。河南省正规划以部分区域重点推动（如中牟县、祥符区、兰考县、原阳县、封丘县、长垣市、濮阳县、范县及台前县等），将滩区移民的原迁地进行广泛种植饲草，并实现科技创新资源的高效融入，将黄河河南滩区建设成为成片优质饲草种植示范和创新技术研发基地。

10 modern agricultural parks.

As an important food production and security area for our country, the Yellow River Basin has made a series of achievements in promoting food safety production, developing water-efficient agriculture, and promoting the bringing up to date and development of green agriculture. It helps fulfill carbon peaking and carbon neutrality goals efficiently through the renovation of agricultural structures and advances the integrated development of primary, secondary, and tertiary industries in rural areas. In the critical period of the 14th Five-Year Plan for national development, it can effectively realize rural revitalization and enhance people's well-being based on ensuring the support of agricultural grain reserves and green development.

VI. Agricultural Development and Achievement of Carbon Peaking and Carbon Neutrality Goals

Agriculture is the key support and guarantee for the development of the Yellow River Basin, and the basin is efficiently achieving the carbon peaking and carbon neutrality goals by optimizing the structure of the agricultural industry and promoting the development of an agricultural carbon market.

(1) Optimizing the structure of the agricultural industry and accelerating the transition to a low-carbon agricultural development mode. Records indicate that in recent years the agricultural carbon emissions along the Yellow River have shown a downward trend, but the intensity of agricultural carbon emissions still has room for further decrease. Based on the differences in regional economic and social structures and development levels among the provinces in the Yellow River Basin, there are regional dissimilarities in agricultural carbon emission intensity among cities in the basin. According to the actual situation, the provinces are introducing relevant policies and measures to reduce the agricultural carbon emission footprint. What is more, a collaborative management center for low-carbon agriculture should actively be established in nine provinces of the Yellow River Basin, and a development plan be formulated for low-carbon agriculture

黄河滩区（兰考县）优质草业带（新华网发,高伟、李春亮摄）
High-quality Grass Belt in the Beach Area of the Yellow River (Lankao County)
(Photographed by Gao Wei and Li Chunliang, Xinhua News Network)

黄河下游入海口处利津县旧村台改造提升工程，提升滩区人民幸福感。为有效实现滩区防洪及安澜的基本要求，多数区域滩区选择迁建方式，以保证滩区人民的生命和财产安全。但部分滩区基于搬迁的较大困难及故土情节，选择直接在滩区原居住地进行就地改造和实地提升，如黄河下游入海口处的利津县实施旧村台改造提升工程，通过居住地面高度提升和排水工程完善，满足下游滩区安澜的基本要求。同时，通过统筹布局及产业融合发展，建立集旅游观光、文化传承和养老休闲为一体的农业发展基地。目前，利津县已成功建成 10 个现代农业园区。

作为我国重要的粮食生产及保障区域，黄河流域在推动粮食安全生产、发展节水农业、促进绿色农业升级发展方面取得了一系列成绩。通过农业结构升级促成“双碳”目标的高效达成，推动农村一二三产业发展融合。在国家“十四五”发展的关键时期，在保障农业粮食储量支撑

under the guidance of the overall development direction, to speedily realize the overall goal of national low-carbon agricultural development.

(2) Actively developing the agricultural carbon market in the Yellow River Basin. Since agriculture has not been included in the carbon market, the provinces in the Yellow River Basin have made full use of the relatively low cost of agricultural carbon emission reduction to include it in the carbon trading market. According to the actual development situation, the key influencing factors on agricultural carbon emissions should first be clarified. In the early stages, in places with a good foundation for green agricultural development, excellent business environments, and sufficient motivation for reform, we can take the county as the organizational unit to select village collective economic organizations, professional industrial farmers, cooperatives, agricultural reclamation or social service organizations, and other large-scale and highly-organized entities with a strong market awareness to take the lead in launching the pilot.

(3) Actively using financial means to promote low-carbon agricultural technology, increasing government investment in agricultural science and technology innovation, and exploring new ideas for low-carbon agricultural development. The Yellow River Basin should establish and improve an agricultural subsidy system and a rural financing system oriented towards green development. The funds of financial support for "agriculture, rural areas, and rural people" should be more closely related to environmental-friendly behavior such as chemical fertilizer and pesticide reduction, straw utilization, plastic film recycling, and land greening, in order to provide incentives for agricultural carbon emissions reduction and carbon sequestration. According to the structure of agricultural carbon emissions, chemical inputs, such as chemical fertilizers and agricultural films, appear to be the main source of carbon emissions. Provinces in the basin should increase their financial support for agricultural science and technology innovation, and promote organic fertilizers instead of chemical ones, soil testing formulas, and other technologies to improve resource utilization efficiency. The Yellow River Basin should increase the use of new energy sources such as light energy and wind energy, and reduce the input of traditional energy sources and the corresponding carbon emissions, intending to effectively realize the use of new energies and material supply in agricultural parks. In the Yellow River Basin, the

及绿色发展的基础上，有效实现乡村振兴及人民幸福发展。

六、农业发展与“双碳”目标达成发展方向

农业作为黄河流域发展的关键支撑和保障，正通过优化农业产业结构、推动发展农业碳市场等途径，实现“双碳”目标的高效达成。

（1）优化农业产业结构，加快推进向低碳农业发展模式的转变。近年来黄河沿岸农业碳排放呈下降趋势，但农业碳排放强度依然存在下降空间。基于流域各省份区域经济社会结构和发展水平的差异，黄河流域各地市农业碳排放强度存在区域差异，各省份正根据实际情况出台相关政策和措施，以提高农业碳减排效率。积极建立黄河流域九省低碳农业协同管理中心，以整体发展方向为指导，制定低碳农业发展计划，尽快实现国家低碳农业发展的整体目标。

（2）积极发展黄河流域农业碳市场。农业尚未纳入碳市场范围，黄河流域各省份充分利用农业减排成本相对较低的优势，将农业碳减排纳入碳交易市场。根据实际发展情况，首先厘清农业碳排放的关键影响因素。初期可在农业绿色发展基础较好、营商环境优良、改革动力足的地方，以县为单位，选择村集体经济组织、专业大户、合作社、农垦、社会化服务组织等规模较大、组织程度较高、市场意识强的主体，率先开展试点。

（3）流域积极利用财政手段推广低碳农业技术，加大政府农业科技创新投入，探索低碳农业发展新思路。黄河流域建立健全以绿色发展为导向的农业补贴制度和农村金融制度，财政和金融支持“三农”的资金进一步密切与化肥农药减量、秸秆利用、地膜回收、国土绿化等环境友好行为的联系程度，为农业减排和固碳持续提供激励。从农业碳排放的结构来看，化肥、农膜等化学投入品是主要碳排放源，流域各省份加大财政对农业科技创新的支持力度，推行有机肥替代化肥、测土配方等技

techniques of minimum tillage and no-tillage ought to be popularized to increase the soil's organic carbon storage. By reducing the tillage range and intensity of farmland use, the basin tries to reduce the physical disturbance of soil, improve soil stability, and increase the proportion of stable soil organic matter in the soil structure. In terms of the application of pesticides and chemical fertilizers, it is advocated to control pests and diseases by biological means, limit the application of chemical fertilizers, and emphasize biological carbon sequestration and organic fertilizer application. The Yellow River Basin should promote carbon sequestration by planting trees, protecting forests, and improving land management. In the catalog of agricultural machinery purchase subsidies, the basin should increase the requirements for energy-saving performance of agricultural machinery, and support the research and development as well as the promotion of energy-saving agricultural equipment.

术，提高资源利用效率。黄河流域强化光能、风能等新能源的使用，减少传统能源的投入及相应碳排放量，有效实现农业园区的新能源使用和物资供给。推广土壤少耕、免耕技术，增加土壤有机碳储量，通过减少农地耕作幅度与强度，尽力减轻土壤的物理性扰动，提高稳定性，增进土壤结构中稳固的土壤有机质比例。在农药和化肥施用方面，提倡用生物学方法控制病虫害，限制化肥的施用量，重视生物固碳和有机肥施用。通过植树造林、保护森林资源、加强土地管理等促进碳固定；在农机购置补贴目录中，增加对农机节能性能的要求，支持节能农机的研发和推广。

第二章

工业高质量发展

Chapter 2

High-quality Development of Industries

黄河流域产业结构整体偏重，9个省（自治区）主导产业多为化工、有色、能源等产业。经评估，“十三五”期间，黄河流域工业高质量发展总指数均值为31.8，与长江流域相比，黄河流域省份工业总量明显不及长江流域，但工业占比高于长江流域。

黄河流域工业目前主要布局在济（南）青（岛）烟（台）为主的山东半岛城市群、郑州为主的中原城市群、西安为主的关中平原城市群以及银川、兰州、西宁等中心城市周边。中上游以能源、化工、有色等材料工业、能源工业为主，中下游以能源、化工、高端装备、轻工为主。因此，在生态保护的发展前提下，产业转型升级成为唯一选择。

一、传统产业转型升级

黄河流域传统产业包括煤炭、钢铁冶炼、石油、轻工纺织、机械制造等。目前，黄河流域的该类传统产业仍然占据着主导地位，是该地区的经济支柱产业，在“双碳”目标和习近平生态文明思想引领下，黄河流域传统产业逐步转型升级。

黄河流域九省区规模以上工业企业按照资产排名为山东省、河南省、四川省、山西省、陕西省、内蒙古、甘肃省、宁夏回族自治区、青海省。其中工业企业总资产排名前3的山东省（9.56万亿元）、河南省（5.27万亿元）和四川省（4.90万亿元）占黄河流域9省区工业企业总资产（33.96万亿元）的58.01%；营业收入山东省（8.32万亿元）、河南省（5.00万亿元）、四川省（4.41万亿元）占黄河流域9省区工业企业营业收入（25.65万亿元）的69.12%。基于各区域的历史发展、资源禀赋及自然条件，黄河流域上游、中游和下游地区的传统产业升级发展存在着显著差异。

依托上游的矿产资源优势，黄河上游的金属冶炼、化工产业占有较大比重。在畜牧业蓬勃发展下，以羊绒纺织、棉纺、麻纺、化纤混纺为

The industrial structure of the Yellow River Basin is dominated by heavy industries, and the leading ones in 9 provinces (autonomous regions) are mainly chemical, non-ferrous, and energy industries. According to the rating, the average overall index of high-quality industrial development in the Yellow River Basin was 31.8 during the 13th Five-Year Plan period. Compared with the Yangtze River Basin, the total industrial output of the provinces in the Yellow River Basin was much lower, but the proportion of industry was higher.

At present, the industry in the Yellow River Basin is mainly concentrated in the Shandong Peninsula urban cluster, represented by Jinan, Qingdao, and Yantai, the Central Plains urban cluster represented by Zhengzhou, the Guanzhong Plain urban cluster represented by Xi'an, as well as the surrounding areas of Yinchuan, Lanzhou, and Xining. The upper and middle portions of the Yellow River are dominated by material industries such as energy, chemicals, and non-ferrous metals, while the middle and lower reaches are dominated by energy, chemicals, high-end equipment, and light industry. Therefore, under the premise of ecological protection, industrial transformation and modernization have become the only choice.

I. Transformation and Upgrades of Traditional Industries

The traditional industries in the Yellow River Basin include coal, steel, petroleum, light industry, textiles, and machinery manufacturing. These industries still occupy a dominant position now and are the pillar of the region. With the goals of achieving carbon peak and carbon neutrality and Xi Jinping's idea of building an ecological civilization, the traditional industries in the Yellow River Basin are gradually transforming and upgrading.

According to a ranking of assets of industrial enterprises above designated size, the nine provinces and regions of the Yellow River Basin are Shandong Province, Henan Province, Sichuan Province, Shanxi Province, Shaanxi Province, Inner Mongolia, Gansu Province, Ningxia Hui Autonomous Region, and Qinghai Province. The top three provinces—Shandong Province (9.56 trillion yuan), Henan Province (5.27 trillion yuan), and Sichuan Province (4.90 trillion yuan)—account for 58.01% of the total assets of industrial enterprises in the nine

主的现代纺织产业也占有关键地位。虽然以资源消耗为主的传统工业方向占比较大，但近年来占比有所下降，以生态发展和绿色循环为主的新能源、新材料、电子信息产品和生物制药等新兴产业增速较快。

宁夏大武口洗煤厂运煤专线
Special Coal Transportation Line of Dawukou Coal Washery in Ningxia

黄河中游地区是典型的资源型地区，煤炭储量高，工业化程度相对较高，矿产资源较为丰富，以煤炭资源为支撑的煤炭化工、能源产业、钢铁冶炼工业是其重要组成部分。重型装备制造业和汽车制造业也是该地区传统产业的主要组成部分。以晋西、智奇、中车太原等轨道交通企业为代表的重型装备制造业和以江铃重汽、比亚迪为代表的汽车工业等是该区域工业的主要组成部分。

provinces and regions in the Yellow River Basin (33.96 trillion yuan). In terms of operating income, Shandong Province (8.32 trillion yuan), Henan Province (5.00 trillion yuan), and Sichuan Province (4.41 trillion yuan) account for 69.12% of the total in the nine provinces and regions of the Yellow River Basin (25.65 trillion yuan). Given different historical development, resources, and natural conditions of each region, there are significant differences in the modernization and development of traditional industries in the upstream, middle, and downstream regions of the Yellow River Basin.

Relying on the advantage of mineral resources, the metal smelting and chemical industries in the upstream region of the Yellow River account for a large proportion. With the prosperous development of animal husbandry, the modern textile industry (mainly composed of cashmere, cotton, hemp, and chemical fiber blending) also plays a key role. Although traditional industries, characterized by resource consumption, still occupy a relatively large share, their percentage has decreased in recent years. Emerging industries such as new energy, new materials, electronic information products, and biopharmaceuticals have been growing rapidly. They focus on ecological development and green circulation.

The middle region of the Yellow River is rich in resources, with large coal reserves and a relatively high degree of industrialization. The coal-chemical industry, energy industry, and steel smelting industry are major economic fields in this region. Heavy equipment manufacturing and automobile manufacturing are also an important part of the traditional industries in this region. Heavy equipment manufacturing, for example, Jinxi Industries Group Co., Ltd., Zhichi Railway Equipment and CRRC Taiyuan Co., Ltd., and the automobile industry represented by Jiangling Motors and BYD are the key partners of the industry in this region.

Located downstream of the Yellow River, Henan Province and Shandong Province are in the leading position in the industrial development of the region. These lower reaches of the Yellow River have large populations and their industrial economies develop rapidly. This region is an important base for steel production in China, providing important raw materials for national economic construction. Non-ferrous metal smelting also occupies an important strategic position. From January to December of 2022, the output of ten kinds of non-ferrous metals in

山西大同煤炭博物馆
Datong Coal Museum, Shanxi

黄河下游河南省和山东省处于流域工业发展的关键引领位置。黄河下游人口众多，工业经济发展迅速。黄河下游是全国重要的钢铁生产基地，为全国经济建设提供了重要的钢铁等原材料的保障。有色金属冶炼也占重要的战略地位，2022 年 1—12 月，河南省规模以上工业企业十种有色金属产量同比增长了 9.7%，达 464.5 万吨，增速较同期全国高 5.4 个百分点。黄河下游的电解铝、铅产量等位居全国前列，如“豫光金铅”“南山铝业”“魏桥铝电”等大型铅业和铝业集团生产的金属制品，均在国内占有重要市场份额。

industrial enterprises above designated size in Henan Province increased by 9.7% year-on-year, reaching 4.645 million tons, a growth rate 5.4 percentages higher than that of the country in the same period. The electrolytic aluminum and lead production in this region is among the top in China. Large lead and aluminum industry groups such as Yuguang Gold Lead Co., Ltd., Nanshan Aluminum Co., Ltd., and Weiqiao Aluminum and Power Co., Ltd. produce metal products that hold important market shares domestically.

In recent years, the provinces and regions on the banks of the Yellow River have actively adjusted their industrial structure and shifted the focus of development towards technology-intensive industries with a higher economic efficiency, striving to achieve the transformation and modernization of traditional industries. In the upper reaches of the Yellow River Basin, efforts are being made to build an important national base for energy, chemicals, and new materials; in the middle reaches, there is a strong push for an energy revolution, focusing on the development of new energy vehicles, high-end equipment manufacturing, and new materials industries; in the lower reaches, the project of replacing old growth drivers with new ones is being implemented, and "specialized, refined, unique, and novel" enterprises are being cultivated to drive industrial transformation and modernization. At the same time, the development of characteristic industry clusters is being promoted to bring the industrial chain to a higher level, so that the transformation and modernization of traditional industries can be achieved.

The manufacturing industry is not only a key engine for revitalizing the real economy and promoting technological innovation, but also a key material guarantee and technical support for the high-quality development of the Yellow River Basin. The development of manufacturing industry in the Yellow River Basin is still dominated by heavy industry, because this area is rich in energy resources and has distinct characteristics of energy-oriented economy.

As the leading provinces of advanced manufacturing in the Yellow River Basin, Henan Province, Shandong Province and Sichuan Province have a high degree of industrialization, a large scale and a good development of advanced manufacturing industry, and therefore they are important bases of advanced manufacturing industry in China with core competitiveness. Shanxi Province, Shaanxi Province and Gansu Province mainly rely on resource-based industries,

山东钢铁集团
Shandong Iron and Steel Group Co., Ltd.

黄河流域各省区近年来对工业结构积极进行调整，发展重心向经济效益更高的技术密集型产业转移，着力于实现传统产业的转型升级。其中，在黄河流域上游地区，致力打造全国重要的能源化工和新材料基地；在中游地区，大力推动能源革命，着力于发展新能源汽车、高端装备制造业和新材料等行业；下游地区，实施新旧动能转换的工程，通过培育“专精特新”企业来带动产业转型升级，同时推动特色产业集群式发展，以此来促进产业链向高端化延伸，以实现传统产业的转型升级。

制造业不仅是振兴实体经济与推动技术创新的关键驱动，也是黄河流域高质量发展的关键物质保障与技术支撑。黄河流域制造业的发展仍以重工业为主，源于黄河流域能源资源丰富，具有鲜明的能源型经济特征。

作为黄河流域先进制造业的领军省份，河南省、山东省和四川省工业化程度较高，先进制造业发展规模较大，发展态势较好，是我国重要的先进制造业基地，具有核心竞争力。山西省、陕西省和甘肃省主要依

and the level of their advanced manufacturing industry has certain potential of improvement. Due to the limitation of ecological conditions, Qinghai Province, Ningxia Hui Autonomous Region, Inner Mongolia and other regions are making steady improvement of advanced manufacturing industry through industrial integration and manufacturing resource allocation.

In recent years, the transformation and upgrading of manufacturing industry in the Yellow River Basin has made great progress and achievements. In the middle and upper reaches of the Yellow River Basin, Qinghai Province, Ningxia Hui Autonomous Region, Gansu Province, Inner Mongolia, Sichuan Province and Shanxi Province are rich in resources and have a large number of traditional enterprises. They attach great importance to ecological and environmental protection in the Yellow River Basin, accelerate the implementation of the major national strategy of ecological protection and high-quality development in the Yellow River Basin, and shut down some traditional enterprises that are high in energy consumption and pollution. The ecological environment in this area has been improved and restored accordingly.

5G自动驾驶公交车

5G Self-driving Bus

靠资源型产业，其先进制造业发展水平具有一定提升空间。青海省、宁夏回族自治区和内蒙古等地区由于生态条件的制约，正通过产业融合布局、制造业资源配置等措施实现先进制造业的稳步提升。

近年来，黄河流域制造业的转型升级取得了较大的进展和成就。黄河流域中上游的青海省、宁夏回族自治区、甘肃省、内蒙古、四川省、山西省资源较为丰富，传统企业数量较多，高度重视黄河流域的生态环境保护，加快推动黄河流域生态保护和高质量发展重大国家战略的实施，关停部分高耗能、高污染的传统企业，该地区生态环境得到了相应的改善和恢复。

黄河流域传统产业的机械制造行业，体现了黄河流域从“中国制造”到“中国创造”的硬实力。位于河南省的中铁工程装备集团利用资源条件，充分发挥中原城市群交通优势，着力推进隧道掘进机（盾构机/TBM）研发制造，打破国外盾构机的技术垄断，实现基础建设“卡脖子”问题的有效解决，产销量连续五年世界第一，出口覆盖五大洲的三十多个国家和地区，成为国内制造的标杆。

二、战略性新兴产业

战略性新兴产业是对经济社会全局和长远发展具有重大引领带动作用的产业，特点是知识技术密集、物质资源消耗少、成长潜力大、综合效益好，是推动高质量发展的重要引擎，是区域未来产业发展的制胜点。《中共中央关于制定国民经济和社会发展第十四个五年规划和二〇三五年远景目标的建议》指出，要以创新驱动发展，加快建设科技

The mechanical manufacturing industry is the traditional industry in the Yellow River Basin, which reflects the hard power of the Yellow River Basin's transitioning from "Made in China" to "Created in China". The China Railway Engineering Equipment Group Co., Ltd., located in Henan Province, fully leverages the advantages of transportation and resources of the Central Plains city cluster, focuses on promoting the research and development and manufacturing of Tunnel Boring Machines (TBM), breaks the technical monopoly of foreign shield machines, effectively solves the "stranglehold" problem of infrastructure construction, and has been the world's largest producer and seller for five consecutive years, with exports covering more than 30 countries and regions on five continents, setting a benchmark for domestic manufacturing.

中铁工程装备集团生产的盾构机

TBM Made by China Railway Engineering Equipment Group Co., Ltd.

II. Strategic Emerging Industries

Strategic emerging industries refer to the ones that play a significant and leading role in the overall and long-term development of the economy and society.

强国，提高企业创新能力，完善科技创新机制，塑造发展优势的发展方向，同时提出“发展战略性新兴产业，构建一批各具特色、优势互补、结构合理的战略性新兴产业增长引擎”。黄河流域正逐步构建战略性新兴产业体系，推动黄河流域的产业协调和高质量发展。

黄河流域科技创新投入及规模以上企业有效发明专利数近年来逐年上涨，通过黄河流域上中下游的差异化优势，对其战略性新兴产业进行定位，实现黄河流域的协同发展，为黄河流域构建战略性新兴产业提供了良好基础。黄河流域沿线的制造业可为构建战略性新兴产业提供基础原材料和各种战略资源的有效支撑。黄河流域拥有多所双一流高校，培养大量战略性新兴产业人才，流域战略性新兴产业的构建可使人才做到人尽其用，避免人才流失。

黄河流域的重点在于发展中下游产业基础较强的地区，建立起战略性新兴产业合作平台，以实现产业的供应与需求之间的有效对接，以及产业上游、中游和下游之间的协同配合，同时紧密衔接产业链、创新链和供应链。这一举措推进了产业体系的升级和基础能力的重新塑造，为打造具有强大竞争力的产业集群提供了有力支撑。黄河流域各省区正创新促进新技术、新产品和新业态、信息技术、航空航天、生物医药、新材料、新能源汽车的发展，提高工业互联网、人工智能、大数据等战略性新兴产业对传统产业渗透率，促进跨界融合创新，为黄河流域战略性新兴产业培育新的经济增长点。

They are characterized by being knowledge-and-technology-intensive, consuming fewer material resources, having great growth potential, and producing good overall benefits. These industries are important engines for promoting high-quality development and they are winners that help the future industrial development of a region. "The Proposal of the Central Committee of the Communist Party of China on Formulating the 14th Five-Year Plan for National Economic and Social Development and the Vision for 2035" points out that innovation should be the driving force for development, and efforts should be made to accelerate the construction of a powerful country in science and technology, enhance the innovative capabilities of enterprises, improve the mechanisms for technological inventions, and shape the direction of competitive advantages. The document also proposes to "develop strategic emerging industries and build a group of strategic growth engines of emerging industries, which are characterized by their unique features, complementary advantages, and reasonable structure". The Yellow River Basin is gradually building a strategic emerging industry system, promoting industrial coordination and high-quality development in the region.

In recent years, investment in scientific and technological innovation and the number of effective invention patents granted to large-scale enterprises in the Yellow River Basin have been increasing year by year. Based on the differentiated advantages of the upper, middle, and lower reaches of the Yellow River Basin, strategic positioning of its emerging industries has been achieved, realizing coordinated development and providing a good foundation for building strategic emerging industries in the region. The manufacturing industry along the Yellow River Basin can provide effective support for the construction of tactical emerging industries by providing basic raw materials and various vital resources. The Yellow River Basin is home to several world-class universities, which have trained many talents for strategic emerging industries. The construction of such industries in this region should maximize the use of talents and avoid the outflow of talents.

The focus of the Yellow River Basin is to develop areas with a strong industrial base in the middle and lower reaches, establish a strategic emerging industry cooperation platform, and realize the effective connection between industrial supply and demand, as well as the coordination between the upstream, midstream and downstream of the industry, meanwhile closely connecting

实施创新工程推动了制造业等战略性新兴产业集群的形成。黄河流域下游地区充分发挥人才优势、雄厚制造业基础优势和城市区位优势，推动了先进制造业的高质量发展，在持续做大规模效益、不断加快动能转换、全面实现数字赋能、逐步增强创新创业活力四个方面取得了显著成绩。

三、能源产业高质量发展

黄河流域能源资源富集，流域的煤炭、石油、天然气和有色金属资源储量丰富，是我国重要的能源、化工、原材料和基础工业基地。以实现“双碳”目标为引领，黄河流域以实现传统能源向新能源转换为落脚点，促进能源现代化发展，增强能源技术创新能力，加快分布式新能源发展。

1. 传统能源支撑

黄河流域的煤炭储量占全国煤炭储量的 50% 以上，2022 年黄河流域的煤炭产量占全国产量的 80% 左右，同时，石油、天然气的产量也都占全国产量的 30% 以上，国家规划的 14 个煤电基地中有 10 个都位于黄河流域。黄河流域是国家能源安全的支柱，有力地支撑了京津冀和华北华中地区的发展。

the industrial chain, innovation chain and supply chain. This initiative has promoted the upgrading of the industrial system and the re-shaping of basic capabilities, providing strong support for building industrial clusters with strong competitiveness. Each province or region in the Yellow River Basin is actively promoting the development of new technologies, new products, and new business models, as well as information technology, aviation and aerospace, biomedicine, new materials, and new energy vehicles. It is also improving the penetration rate of strategic emerging industries such as industrial internet, artificial intelligence, and big data in traditional industries, promoting cross-border integration and innovation, and cultivating new economic growth points for strategic emerging industries in the Yellow River Basin.

The implementation of innovation projects has promoted the formation of strategic emerging industrial clusters such as manufacturing industry. The lower reaches of the Yellow River Basin have given full play to their advantages in human resources, strong manufacturing base and urban location, promoted the high-quality development of advanced manufacturing, and made remarkable achievements in the four aspects of sustained large-scale efficiency, accelerating the transformation of kinetic energy, fully realizing digital empowerment, and gradually enhancing the vitality of innovation and entrepreneurship.

III. High-quality Development of Energy Industry

The Yellow River Basin is rich in energy resources, with abundant reserves of coal, oil, natural gas, and non-ferrous metals, making it an important base for energy, chemical, raw material, and basic industries in China. To achieve the targets of carbon peak and carbon neutralization, the Yellow River Basin takes the transformation from traditional energy to new energy as the starting point, promotes the modernization of energy development, enhances energy technological innovation capabilities, and further develops the distribution of new energy.

1. Support from Traditional Energy Suppliers

The coal reserves in the Yellow River Basin account for more than 50% of China's total coal reserves, and the coal production in the Yellow River Basin in

黄河流经甘肃、宁夏、内蒙古、陕西和山西五省区的“几”字地带是黄河流域乃至全国重要的能源产地，其能源产出大部分为化石能源，为全国经济发展提供了源源不断的动力。陕西省煤炭、石油、天然气储量均名列前茅，2022 年原煤产量 74604.5 万吨，位居全国第四；原油产量 2536.6 万吨，位居全国第三；天然气产量 307.3 亿立方米，位居全国第三。山西省是全国最大的煤炭生产大省，原煤的年产量达到了 10 亿吨以上，拥有晋北、晋中和晋东三个大型煤炭基地。我国第一大油田长庆油田分布在陕西、甘肃、宁夏、内蒙古、山西五省区的 15 个地市，拥有石油总资源量 85.88 亿吨，天然气总资源量 10.7 万亿立方米，同时还蕴藏着丰富的煤炭、岩盐、煤层气、铀等资源。

目前，黄河流域内已经建成九大煤炭基地、六大煤电基地、多个石油天然气生产基地、煤层气勘探开发基地。黄河流域的能源支撑了全国经济发展，为其提供了强大动力，对保障我国能源安全具有重大意义。

2. 新能源引领

黄河流域上游地区是我国风能和太阳能丰富的地区之一。风能资源开发潜力占全国一半以上，太阳能资源主要为Ⅰ类和Ⅱ类区域，其中内蒙古额济纳旗以西、甘肃酒泉以西、青海湖以西属于极丰富带。太阳能资源丰富，主要分布在西北及华北地区，上中游的青海、甘肃、宁夏、内蒙古、山西大部分属Ⅰ类地区和Ⅱ类地区。内蒙古的风能、太阳能资

2022 makes up around 80% of the national production. Moreover, the production of oil and natural gas also constitutes more than 30% of the national production. Ten of the 14 coal-fired power plants scheduled by the country are located in the Yellow River Basin which is the pillar of China's energy security and provides strong support for the development of the Beijing-Tianjin-Hebei, the North, and Central China regions.

The "几" -shaped area that covers the Gansu, Ningxia, Inner Mongolia, Shaanxi, and Shanxi provinces and regions, through which the Yellow River flows, is an important energy-producing area in the Yellow River Basin and even the whole country, with fossil energy taking up most of the energy production. It provides a steady stream of power for the national economic development. Shaanxi Province has abundant reserves of coal, oil, and natural gas, with the coal production of 746.045 million tons in 2022, ranking fourth in the country; its crude oil production is 25.366 million tons, ranking third in China; the natural gas production is 30.73 billion cubic meters, ranking third in China. Shanxi Province is the largest coal-producing province in China, with an annual coal production of over 1 billion tons and 3 large coal mines in the north, middle, and east of the province. The largest oil field in China, the Changqing Oil Field, spreads over 15 cities in Shaanxi, Gansu, Ningxia, Inner Mongolia, and Shanxi provinces and regions, with a total oil resource of 8.588 billion tons and a total natural gas resource of 10.7 trillion cubic meters, as well as abundant resources of coal, rock salt, coal-bed methane, and uranium.

At present, nine large coal mines, six coal-fired power bases, and several oil and gas production bases and coal-bed methane exploration and development bases have been established in the Yellow River Basin. The energy in this basin supports national economic development, provides a strong impetus for it, and is of great importance in ensuring China's energy security.

2. The Leading Role of New Energy

The upper reaches of the Yellow River Basin are among the richest regions in China for wind and solar energy. The potential of wind energy resources accounts for more than half of the country, while solar energy resources are mainly concentrated in Class I and Class II regions. The western regions beyond Ejin Banner in Inner Mongolia, Jiuquan in Gansu, and Qinghai Lake

源较为丰富，“十三五”以来，内蒙古建成了全国规模最大的新能源基地。2021年，内蒙古锡林郭勒盟建成内蒙古首个千万千瓦级清洁能源基地。同时，内蒙古太阳能资源富足，日照时间长，太阳能资源仅次于西藏，位居全国第二位。甘肃省风能资源丰富，有效储量为2.37亿千瓦，全国排名第五，且太阳能资源非常丰富，太阳能技术可开发量在1亿千瓦以上，全国排名第三。目前，黄河流域内已建成多个水电基地、光伏发电领跑基地，推动了我国能源的清洁转型升级。

黄河流域风能发电

Wind Power Generation in the Yellow River Basin

are considered the best areas by far for solar energy. The abundant solar energy resources are mainly distributed in Northwest and North China, with Qinghai, Gansu, Ningxia, Inner Mongolia, and Shanxi in the upper and middle reaches being Class I and Class II areas. Inner Mongolia has relatively great potential for wind and solar energy solutions. Since the 13th Five-Year Plan, Inner Mongolia has built the largest new energy base in the country. In 2021, Xiliin Gol League in Inner Mongolia completed the first clean energy plant with a capacity of 10 million kilowatts in the region. Meanwhile, Inner Mongolia has abundant solar energy resources, ranking second in the country after Tibet, with long sunshine hours. Gansu Province is also rich in wind energy resources, with an effective storage capacity of 237 million kilowatts, ranking fifth in the country, and its solar energy resources are also very abundant, with a potential technical capacity of over 100 million kilowatts, taking third place in the country. Currently, multiple hydropower facilities and photovoltaic power generation leading bases have been established in the Yellow River Basin, promoting the clean transition and upgrading of China's energy supply.

As the pillar industry of the economy in the Yellow River Basin, traditional industries are gradually transforming and upgrading. The manufacturing industry, mainly heavy industry manufacturing, is based on ample energy resources in the Yellow River Basin and has distinct energy-economic characteristics, making significant achievements in transformation and modernization. Meanwhile, a strategic emerging industry system is gradually being put in place, promoting industrial coordination and top-level development in the Yellow River Basin. To achieve targets of carbon peak and carbon neutralization, the basin is leading the transitioning from traditional energy to new energy, enhancing its energy technology innovation capabilities, and speedily develops the distribution of new energy.

黄河流域传统产业作为经济支柱产业，正在逐步转型升级；制造业以重工业为主，主要源于黄河流域拥有丰富的能源资源，具有鲜明的能源型经济特征，转型升级取得了较大的成就；同时逐步构建战略性新兴产业体系，推动黄河流域的产业协调和高质量发展；最后，以实现“双碳”目标为引领，黄河流域实现传统能源向新能源转换，增强能源技术创新能力，加快分布式新能源发展。

四、现存问题

（1）黄河流域的产业结构存在改进的必要，创新能力尚需进一步加强，同时也需要解决同质化问题，提升城市发展的动力。目前，黄河流域的产业结构呈现出第二产业比重较大的特点，主要由传统制造业和资源型产业占据主导地位。虽然这些产业在过去对当地经济的推动发挥了重要作用，但也带来了环境压力和资源消耗问题。与之相对，高新技术产业、先进制造业和现代服务业的比重较低，限制了黄河流域在新兴产业领域的发展。然而，与长江流域的一些城市相比，目前黄河流域的城市在创新能力和开放程度上还存在一定的不足，这导致流域内新技术、创新人才和资本等要素的吸引力相对较弱。

（2）产业抑制与黄河流域现代产业自我发展滞后。在黄河流域，特别是西部地区，大量外来产业的涌入使得本地产业在竞争中处于相对劣势地位，难以与外来产业形成有力的竞争优势，从而出现了产业抑制的现象。产业抑制给黄河流域，特别是西部地区带来了一系列后果。首先，由于外来产业往往在本地进行简单的组装和生产，而高附加值的环节和关键技术往往掌握在外部，这导致黄河流域产业链的上游与外部的关联过于薄弱。其次，由于外来产业与本地产业在技术水平、管理经验等方面存在差距，导致两者之间的产业链衔接不紧密，产业间的协同效应受到抑制，产业发展出现割裂和碎片化现象。由于这种产业抑制现

IV. Current Challenges

(1) The industrial structure of the Yellow River Basin needs to be improved, the innovation capacity needs to be further strengthened, the problem of homogenization needs to be solved and the driving force of urban development needs to be improved. At present, the industrial structure of the Yellow River Basin is characterized by a large proportion of secondary industry, mainly dominated by traditional manufacturing and resource-based industries. While these industries have played an important role in boosting the local economy in the past, they have also brought problems related to the environment and resource consumption. In contrast, the proportion of high-tech industries, advanced manufacturing and modern service industries is relatively low, which limits the development of new industries in the Yellow River Basin. However, compared with some cities in the Yangtze River Basin, the cities in the Yellow River Basin still have some shortcomings in innovation ability and openness, which leads to the relatively weak attraction of new technologies, innovative talents and capital.

(2) There exists industrial inhibition and the development of modern industry is still backward. In the Yellow River Basin, especially in the west region of it, the influx of a large number of external industries makes the local industries in a relatively inferior position in the competition, and it is difficult for them to form a strong competitive advantage. This problem has brought a series of consequences to the Yellow River Basin, especially to the west region. First, as the external industries in the Yellow River Basin areas often undertake simple assembly and production, not bringing in high value-added links and key technologies, the upstream industrial chain of the Yellow River Basin has weak connection with the external. Second, due to the gap between the external and local industries in terms of technical level and management, the industrial chain between the two is not so close, the synergistic effect between them is suppressed, and the development of industries is separated and fragmented. As a result, the independent development of modern industries such as modern producer service industry, advanced manufacturing industry and processing manufacturing industry in the Yellow River Basin has been hindered, and the industrial specialization has been restricted.

象，黄河流域现代生产性服务业、先进制造业、加工制造业等现代产业的自主发展受到了阻碍，制约了黄河流域产业分工的形成。

五、解决路径

（1）为实现黄河流域产业的可持续发展，首要任务是完善城市分工协作的产业分工路径。这需要实现产业发展方式由“外生导入”向“内生发展”的根本性转变。目前，黄河流域主要依赖外部要素，如资本、技术和人才的引入，而缺乏自主创新和自我驱动的能力，因此，重要的一步是培育本地的现代化产业，使其成为推动经济发展的核心引擎。依托济南、青岛、郑州、西安等科研资源丰富、科技实力雄厚的中心城市，黄河流域可以迅速发展新的产业竞争优势，加快经济转型升级的步伐，在这些中心城市的引领下，黄河流域可以采取一系列战略措施，大力发展现代产业集聚区和产业基地，从而全面推动地区经济的蓬勃发展。构建以现代生产性服务业、先进制造业、新兴产业、加工制造业等为主体的产业分工体系是黄河流域产业结构优化和转型升级的关键举措。这样的产业分工体系将促进各类产业的协同发展，推动经济的多元化发展。

（2）以创新驱动为动力，是推动黄河流域产业结构转型升级和建立现代化产业体系的核心策略。在全面落实创新驱动发展战略的基础上，需要采取一系列措施，不断激发创新活力、提升产业竞争力。目前，黄河流域的发展方式仍然相对粗放，这一现状导致产业结构中传统制造业和资源型产业占比较大，而高新技术产业、先进制造业和现代服务业的比重相对较低，产业同质化现象严重，对区域经济的长远发展构成了潜在风险。在新时代的发展形势下，黄河流域城市要实现高质量发展，必须以创新为引领，加速推动新旧动能转换，积极培育新兴产业，推进产业结构转型升级，实现产城融合，构筑现代化产业体系。过去，黄河流

V. Feasible Solutions

(1) In order to achieve sustainable industrial development in the Yellow River Basin, the priority is to improve the path of industrial division under the division of work and cooperation among cities. This requires a fundamental change in the mode of industrial development from "exogenous introduction" to "endogenous development". At present, the Yellow River Basin mainly relies on external factors, such as the introduction of capital, technology and talents, but lacks the capacity for independent innovation and self-drive, so it is important to cultivate the local modern industry and make it a core engine to drive economic development. The Yellow River Basin can rapidly develop new industrial competitive advantages and accelerate the pace of economic transformation and upgrading, relying on Jinan, Qingdao, Zhengzhou, Xi 'an and other central cities which have rich scientific research resources and strong scientific and technological strength. Under the guidance of these central cities, the Yellow River Basin can adopt a series of strategic measures to develop modern industrial clusters and industrial bases vigorously, thus comprehensively promoting the dynamic development of regional economy. Building an industrial division system with modern producer service industry, advanced manufacturing industry, emerging industry and processing manufacturing industry as the main body is a key measure to optimize, transform and upgrade the industrial structure in the Yellow River Basin. Such a system will promote the coordinated development of various industries and promote the diversified development of the economy.

(2) Innovation-driven is the core strategy to promote the transformation and upgrading of industrial structure and the establishment of a modern industrial system in the Yellow River Basin.On the basis of fully implementing the innovation-driven development strategy, a series of measures need to be taken to continuously stimulate innovation vitality and enhance industrial competitiveness. At present, the mode of development in the Yellow River Basin is still relatively extensive, which leads to the large proportion of traditional manufacturing and resource-based industries in the industrial structure, while the proportion of high-tech industries, advanced manufacturing and modern service industries is relatively low, so that industrial homogeneity is serious, posing potential risks to the long-

域的发展主要依赖资源密集型的“三高”工业，虽然这些产业在一定程度上推动了当地经济发展，但也带来了资源浪费和环境压力等问题，因此不再适应当前经济发展的需求。因此，转向依靠技术创新的“三低”绿色工业成了必然选择。

term development of regional economy. In the new era, the cities in the Yellow River Basin must take innovation as the guide, accelerate the transformation of old and new driving forces, actively cultivate emerging industries, promote the transformation and upgrading of industrial structure, realize the integration of industry and city, and build a modern industrial system, so as to achieve high-quality development. In the past, the development of the Yellow River Basin mainly relied on "three high" resource-intensive industries. Although these industries promoted local economic development to a certain extent, they brought about problems to the resources and environment. Therefore, they no longer meet the needs of economic development at present. Turning to the "three low" green industry that relies on technological innovation has become an inevitable choice.

第三章

服务业高质量发展

Chapter 3

High-quality Development of Service Industry

黄河流域服务业高质量发展可高效推动贯彻落实黄河重大国家战略，随着互联网技术、高科学技术以及金融手段等数字经济的迅速发展，不仅可以为黄河流域传统行业提供创新手段，也可以有效实现行业的转型升级。

一、服务业发展概况

在黄河流域，2022年服务业增加值超万亿的省区有四川、山西、陕西、河南和山东，分别为2.93万亿、1.04万亿、1.40万亿、2.96万亿和4.55万亿；四川、甘肃、山东三省的服务业增加值占地区生产总值的比重均超过50%。甘肃、内蒙古第三产业增加值处于黄河流域9省区中游水平，增加值分别为0.57万亿和0.92万亿。青海与宁夏增加值相对较低，分别为0.16万亿元和0.22万亿元。

表 3-1 黄河流域服务产业值及比重（2022 年）

省区	分行业增加值 / 亿元							
	批发和零售业	交通、运输、仓储	住宿和餐饮业	金融业	房地产业	其他	增加值	占地区生产总值比重
青海	171.1	155.2	34.6	286.2	145	847.3	1639.4	45.41%
四川	5132.1	1587.5	1180.1	3840.1	3446	14130.1	29315.9	51.66%
甘肃	795.6	555.6	155.1	925.1	573.2	2681	5685.6	50.76%
宁夏	218.8	213.5	54.1	352.2	185.1	1166.2	2189.9	43.20%
内蒙古	1585.3	1317.9	291.7	981.7	830.3	4200	9206.9	39.76%
山西	1666.7	1198.5	213.8	1359	1165.5	4771.7	10375.2	40.46%
陕西	2103.3	1293.8	400.8	2109.7	1617.9	6485.2	14010.7	42.75%
河南	4496.5	3721.1	1066.5	3301.4	3631	13414.5	29631	48.30%
山东	11819.1	4911	1276.2	5203.1	4406.7	17886.6	45502.7	52.04%

在 2021 年《中国城市服务业高质量发展前 30 强城市》报告排行榜中，四川省成都市服务业高质量发展指数 19.041，排名第 13；陕西省西安市服务业高质量发展指数 13.888，排名第 22；河南省郑州市服务业高质量发展指数 16.937，排名第 17；山东省济南市服务业高质量发展指数 13.865，排名第 23，充分体现了黄河流域内成都、西安、郑州、

A high-quality development of the service industry in the Yellow River Basin can effectively promote the implementation of major national strategies related to the Yellow River. With the rapid development of the digital economy, such as internet technology, high-tech technology, and financial tools, it can not only provide innovative means for traditional industries in the Yellow River Basin, but also achieve the transformation and bringing up to date of the industry.

I. Overview of Service Industry Development

In the Yellow River Basin, there were five provinces whose added value of the service industry exceeded one trillion yuan in 2022, namely Sichuan, Shanxi, Shaanxi, Henan, and Shandong, with values of 2.93 trillion yuan, 1.04 trillion yuan, 1.40 trillion yuan, 2.96 trillion yuan, and 4.55 trillion yuan respectively. The proportion of the added value of the service industry to the regional GDP in Sichuan, Gansu, and Shandong provinces all exceeded 50%. The added value of the tertiary industry in Gansu and Inner Mongolia is at the middle level among the nine provinces and regions in the Yellow River Basin, with values of 0.57 trillion yuan and 0.92 trillion yuan respectively. Qinghai and Ningxia have relatively low added value, with values of 0.17 trillion yuan and 0.21 trillion yuan in the order given.

济南等中心城市和城市群在服务业发展方面的成效，助推了黄河流域整体服务业高质量发展，进一步彰显了黄河流域发展生活性服务业的重要地位。

1. 交通、运输、仓储业发展

黄河流域公路铁路交通具有较好的基础条件，作为经济发展的重要先导，随着跨河交通及黄河重大国家战略的推进，黄河流域交通、运输、仓储业发展迅速，建立了一大批国家级物流示范园区，并基于地区优势资源及物产特征，形成了集交易平台、加工、储存、运输于一体的交通、运输、仓储融合平台。从 2022 年黄河流域的交通、运输、仓储业增值结果分析，其所占第三产业总体产值的比例为 10.1%。黄河下游的河南省、山东省明显高于黄河上、中游的省区。上游青海省增值为 155.2 亿元，中游山西省增值为 1198.5 亿元，下游河南省和山东省的增值则分别达 3721.1 亿元和 4911 亿元。

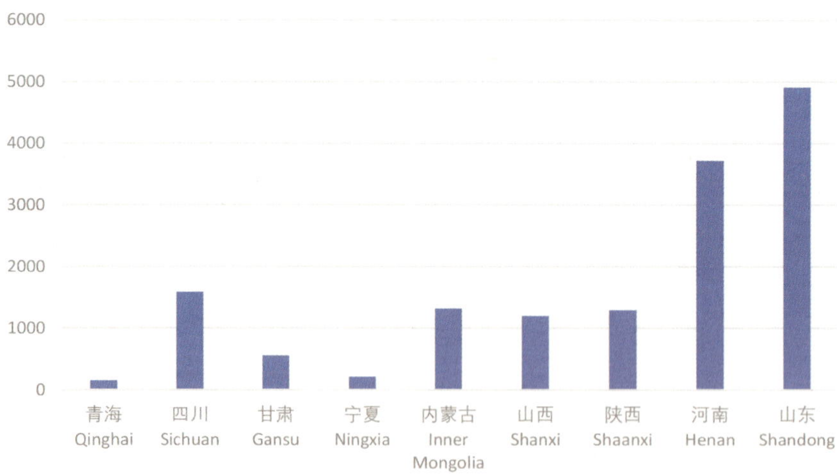

黄河流域各省区2022年交通、运输、仓储业增值（亿元）

Added Value of Transportation ,Logistics and Warehousing Industries in the Provinces and Regions of the Yellow River Basin in 2022 (Hundred million/Yuan)

Table 3-1 Output Value and Proportion of Service Industry in the Yellow River Basin (2022)

Provinces and regions	Value added by industry/100 million yuan							
	Wholesale and retail	Transportation logistics and warehousing	Accommodation and catering	Finance	Real estate	Others	Added value	Proportion in regional GDP
Qinghai	171.1	155.2	34.6	286.2	145	847.3	1639.4	45.41%
Sichuan	5132.1	1587.5	1180.1	3840.1	3446	14130.1	29315.9	51.66%
Gansu	795.6	555.6	155.1	925.1	573.2	2681	5685.6	50.76%
Ningxia	218.8	213.5	54.1	352.2	185.1	1166.2	2189.9	43.20%
Inner Mongolia	1585.3	1317.9	291.7	981.7	830.3	4200	9206.9	39.76%
Shanxi	1666.7	1198.5	213.8	1359	1165.5	4771.7	10375.2	40.46%
Shaanxi	2103.3	1293.8	400.8	2109.7	1617.9	6485.2	14010.7	42.75%
Henan	4496.5	3721.1	1066.5	3301.4	3631	13414.5	29631	48.30%
Shandong	11819.1	4911	1276.2	5203.1	4406.7	17886.6	45502.7	52.04%

In the "Top 30 Cities for High-Quality Development of China's Urban Service Industry in 2021" report, Chengdu of Sichuan Province has a high-quality development index of the service industry of 19.041, ranking 13th; Xi'an of Shaanxi Province has an index of 13.888, ranking 22nd; Zhengzhou of Henan Province has an index of 16.937, taking 17th place, and Jinan of Shandong Province has an index of 13.685, ranking 23rd. This fully reflects the effectiveness of central cities and urban clusters such as Chengdu, Xi'an,Zhengzhou, and Jinan in the development of the service industry in the Yellow River Basin, which has promoted a high-quality development of the service industry in the whole region and further highlighted the important position of the development of living services in the Yellow River Basin.

1. The Development of Transportation, Logistics, and Warehousing Industry

The Yellow River Basin has good infrastructure for highway and railway transportation. As an important engine of economic development, the transportation, logistics, and warehousing industry in the Yellow River Basin have developed rapidly, supported by the promotion of cross-river transportation and the implementation of major national strategies related to the Yellow River. A

2. 金融业发展

黄河流域金融行业发展迅速，是服务业发展的龙头力量，也是带动经济前进的关键行业。黄河流域正大力推动数字经济的持续发展，实现其在各层次城市的融合发展。在推动黄河流域高质量发展过程中，正逐步发挥金融业的支持作用，高效选择金融业的优先支持方向，优先支持实体经济，充分支持高效生态产业和现代高效农业两大体系。从 2022 年黄河流域金融业增值结果分析，其所占第三产业总体产值的比例为 12.4%。下游的河南省、山东省高于黄河上、中游的大部分省区，上游青海省增值为 286.2 亿元，中游山西省增值为 1359 亿元，下游河南省和山东省的增值则分别达 3301.4 亿元和 5203.1 亿元。除四川省外，黄河中上游省区仍需强化金融业的优化发展。

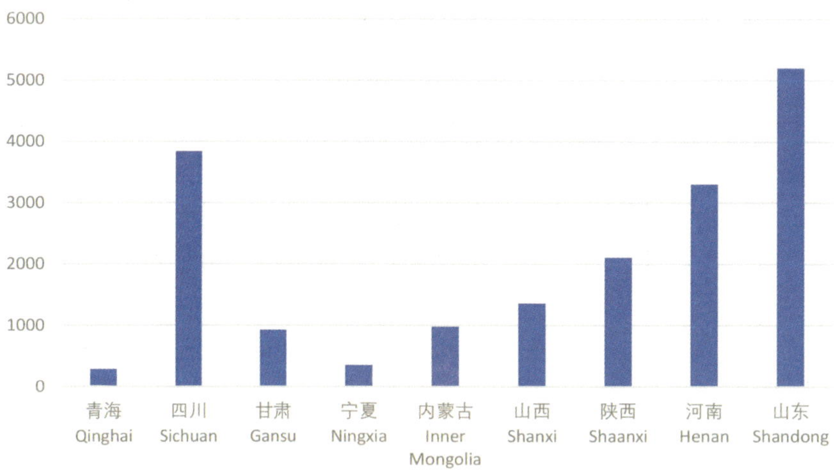

黄河流域各省区2022年金融业增值（亿元）

Added Value of Financial Industry in the Provinces and Regions of the Yellow River Basin in 2022 (Hundredmillion/Yuan)

large number of national-level logistics demonstration parks have been established, and—based on regional resource advantages and product characteristics—integrated transportation, logistics, and warehousing platforms have been formed that combine trading platforms, processing, storage, and transportation. In 2022, the added value of the transportation, logistics, and warehousing industry in the Yellow River Basin accounted for 10.1% of the overall output of the tertiary industry. Henan Province and Shandong Province, located downstream of the Yellow River, have significantly higher values than the provinces and regions located upstream or in the middle reaches. The added value for Qinghai Province of the upper reaches was 15.52 billion yuan, and for Shanxi Province of the middle reaches was 119.85 billion yuan, while for downstream provinces such as Henan and Shandong, the added value was 372.11 billion yuan and 491.1 billion yuan respectively.

2. Development of the Financial Industry

The financial industry in the Yellow River Basin has developed rapidly and it is a leading force in the service industry, playing a critical role in driving economic growth. The Yellow River Basin is vigorously promoting the continuous development of the digital economy and achieving its integrated development at all levels of cities. In the process of promoting high-quality development of the Yellow River Basin, the financial industry is gradually playing a supporting role by efficiently selecting priority areas for financial support, prioritizing support for the real economy, and fully supporting the two major systems of ecological industry and modern and efficient agriculture. In 2021, the added value of the financial industry in the Yellow River Basin constituted 12.4% of the overall output of the tertiary industry. Downstream provinces such as Henan and Shandong have higher values than most provinces and regions located upstream or in the middle reaches of the Yellow River. The added value for Qinghai Province in the upper reaches was 28.62 billion yuan, and for Shanxi Province in the middle reaches was 135.9 billion yuan, while for downstream provinces such as Henan and Shandong, the added value was 330.14 billion yuan and 520.31 billion yuan respectively. Except for Sichuan, provinces and regions in the middle and upper reaches of the Yellow River still need to strengthen the optimization and development of their

3. 文化旅游产业发展

文化旅游产业作为生活性服务业的重要组成部分，也是推动黄河流域生态保护和高质量发展的先导产业。黄河流域拥有丰富的文化资源和旅游资源，其中，国家全域旅游示范区 47 个、国家级旅游度假区 9 个、不可移动文物 30 余万处、国家 5A 级旅游景区 84 个、国家级非遗代表性项目 649 项、全国红色旅游经典景区 85 个、全国乡村旅游重点村 39 个等。2019 年沿黄地区的旅游业总收入达到 55759.63 亿元，相较于 2017 年沿黄地区旅游业总收入的 40232.44 亿元，提高了 38.6 个百分点；文化和体育业总收入在 2019 年到达了 3817.49 亿元，同比 2017 年提高 5.11%。黄河流域以生态和文化资源丰富为先天优势，以促进文化旅游产业高质量发展为理念，打造黄河文化精品旅游带，为黄河流域生活性服务业高质量发展提供了坚实支撑。

黄河流域下游的孔子博物馆

The Confucius Museum in the Lower Reaches of the Yellow River Basin

financial industry.

3. Development of the Cultural Tourism Industry

As an important component of the life-service industry, the cultural tourism industry is also a leading industry that promotes ecological protection and high-quality development of the Yellow River Basin. This region has abundant cultural and tourism resources, including 47 national demonstration zones for tourism, 9 national tourist resorts, over 300,000 immovable cultural antiquities, 84 national 5A-level tourist attractions, 649 national intangible cultural heritage projects, 85 national red tourism classic scenic spots, and 39 national key rural tourism villages. In 2019, the total tourism revenue in the Yellow River region reached 5575.963 billion yuan, an increase of 38.6 percentage points compared to 4023.244 billion yuan in 2017. The total revenue of the culture and sports industry reached 381.749 billion yuan in 2019, a year-on-year increase of 5.11% from 2017. With its inherent advantages in rich ecological and cultural resources, the Yellow River Basin takes the promotion of high-quality development of the cultural tourism industry as its guiding principle and creates a series of high-quality tourism products to support the high-quality development of the life-service industry in the region.

4. Service Industry Development of Typical Provinces

Take Henan Province as a typical example of the Yellow River Basin. In 2020 and 2021, Henan carried out pilot projects on the integrated development of the modern service industry and advanced manufacturing industry, and vigorously cultivated about 50 provincial-level integrated development pilot projects and 100 service-oriented manufacturing demonstration enterprises. With modern service industry development zones and advanced manufacturing industry development zones as its basis, a group of deeply integrated enterprise platforms has been created, exploring new paths, new formats, and new models for the high-quality development of the industry. The added value of the service industry in Henan Province accounted for 49.14% of GDP, and the added value of the production-oriented service industry made up 39.4% of the service industry, with the highest level of production-oriented service industry development in the Yellow River Basin. Among them, the level of development of three industries—namely, information transmission, software and information technology services,

4. 典型省份服务业发展

以黄河流域典型省份河南省为例，河南省于2020年和2021年先后开展了现代服务业和先进制造业的融合发展试点，大力培育了50个左右省级以上融合发展试点和100个左右服务型制造示范企业，以现代服务业开发区和先进制造业开发区为依托，打造了一批深度融合型企业平台，为产业高质量发展探索了新路径、新业态和新模式。河南省服务业增加值占GDP比重为49.14%，生产性服务业增加值占服务业比重为39.4%，其生产性服务业发展水平在黄河流域中最高。其中，信息传输、软件和信息技术服务业，租赁和商务服务业等两个行业发展水平同比其他七个省份发展水平最高，2021年1—6月，信息传输、软件和信息技术服务业实现业务收入639.55亿元，同比增长18.4%，拉动规模以上服务业增长3.4个百分点；租赁和商务服务业实现业务收入471.04亿元，同比增长6.1%。

作为承东启西和纵贯南北的交通枢纽大省，河南省具有“十横十纵”五条综合交通大道的地理位置，以及新郑国际机场、“米”字型铁路枢纽等。被评为中国会展名城，办展数量居全国前列，郑州国家中心城市建设、郑州航空港经济综合实验区、河南自由贸易试验区、郑洛新国家自主创新区、跨境电子商务综合试验区等国家战略规划在河南开展。以郑州为中心的两小时经济圈覆盖4亿人口，具有显著的消费市场优势。河南省充分发挥与山东省的联合联动机制，将生产性服务业与先进制造业的发展进行深度融合，进一步提高了服务“稳”的基础和“进”的功能，为河南省融入“国内国际双循环”发展格局提供了坚实的保障和支撑。

二、现代服务业及体系优化提升方向

构建科技、绿色、供应链等多元金融体系。金融业作为黄河流域服

and leasing and business services—was the highest compared to the other seven provinces. From January to June 2021, the business revenue of the information transmission, software, and information technology services industry reached 63.955 billion yuan, a year-on-year increase of 18.4%, driving the growth of the scale of the service industry above the designated size by 3.4 percentage points. The business revenue of the leasing and business service industry reached 47.104 billion yuan, an annual increase of 6.1%.

As a transportation hub province that connects the east and the west, and runs through the north and the south, Henan Province is located at the intersection of "Ten Horizontal and Ten Vertical" comprehensive transportation arteries, with facilities such as the Xinzheng International Airport, the "米"-shaped railway hub and so on. It has been named a Chinese convention and exhibition city, with exhibition quantity ranking at the top of the country. National strategic plans such as the construction of Zhengzhou as a national central city, the Zhengzhou Airport Economy Zone, the Henan Pilot Free Trade Zone, the Zhengzhou-Luoyang New National Independent Innovation Demonstration Zone, and the Comprehensive Pilot Zone for Cross-border E-commerce have all been implemented in Henan Province. The two-hour economic circle centered on Zhengzhou covers a population of 400 million, providing significant advantages in consumer markets. Henan Province has fully utilized the joint linkage mechanism with Shandong Province to deepen the integration of productive services and advanced manufacturing, further enhancing the foundation of "stability" and the function of "progress" in services, providing solid support and a guarantee for Henan Province to integrate into the "dual circulation" development pattern both domestically and internationally.

II.Direction of Optimization for Modern Service Industry and System

The construction of diversified financial systems of technology, green, and supply chains is being established. As the industry with the largest proportion of development in the service sector of the Yellow River Basin, there are still certain gaps in the financial industry transitioning process toward the perfect modern service industry system. Therefore, the Yellow River Basin is gradually establishing

务业中发展比重最大的行业，与现代服务业产业体系完善仍有一定差距。因此，黄河流域正逐步建立多元金融主体，将企业融资渠道扩大，将更多资金吸引到黄河流域之中。健全企业融资服务帮扶与导向机制。同时，要把握绿色、科技、供应链等新兴行业的发展机会。健全推动黄河流域股权交易中心的发展，推动黄河流域商品交易所创新发展是必然要求。构建多元化渠道、规范化制度金融服务系统，推进区域金融服务平台的建设，提高融资服务的监管。

加强现代服务业与制造业深度融合。制造业作为黄河流域经济发展建设的关键力量，正进一步与现代服务业进行融合发展。大力发展面向制造业企业高新技术服务业，加大对研究设计、信息安全、技术咨询等生产性技术服务的政策优化支持力度，建设智能工厂、数字化车间等先进制造示范企业。同时，黄河流域大力发展服务业外部产业和工业软件，鼓励和支持制造企业自主发展软件开发，向专业化方向发展制造过程。

加强品牌建设能力，提高服务质量。品牌建设是体现区域竞争力的综合体现，是顺应制造业服务化、消费多元化、个性多元化的发展趋势，促进生产服务业向专业化、价值链上移、高端化、精细化、精品化扩展，是黄河流域建设区域性服务中心，促进服务业加快扩张规模、提升质量的综合体现。把绿色发展理念贯穿于服务业体系，提升服务质量，提升服务业体系，坚持以百姓需求为导向，顺应百姓对高品质生活

diversified financial entities to expand enterprise financing channels and attract more funds into the region. The support and guidance mechanisms for enterprise financing services will be improved. At the same time, opportunities for the development of emerging industries such as green, technology, and supply chains will be seized. It is essential to improve the development of the Yellow River Basin equity trading center and promote the innovative development of the Yellow River Basin commodity exchange. A diversified and standardized financial service system will be constructed to advance the construction of a regional financial service platform and enhance the supervision of financing services.

The deep integration of the modern service industry and manufacturing will be strengthened. As a key force in the economic development of the Yellow River Basin, manufacturing is further integrated with the modern service industry. Efforts will be made to develop high-tech service industries for manufacturing enterprises and increase policy optimization support for production technology services such as research and design, information security, and technical consultation. Advanced manufacturing demonstration enterprises, such as intelligent factories and digital workshops, will be built. Meanwhile, the Yellow River Basin will vigorously develop external service industries and industrial software, encouraging and supporting manufacturing enterprises to develop software and information departments independently and to move towards a specialized direction in the manufacturing process.

The ability to build brands will be strengthened, and service quality will be improved. Brand building is a comprehensive reflection of regional competitiveness, which is in line with the development trend of manufacturing services, consumer diversification, and individualization. It promotes the extension of the production service industry towards specialization, value chain upgrading, a high-end focus, refinement, and quality. It is a comprehensive reflection of the construction of a regional service center to promote the accelerated expansion and quality improvement of the service industry. Green development concepts will be incorporated into the service industry system to enhance service quality, adhere to people's needs as the main orientation, meet people's expectations for high-quality living, prioritize quality, and satisfy people's consumption upgrading. In the process of improving the quality of life, green development concepts will be implemented throughout the development of the service industry.

的期待，坚持质量第一，满足百姓消费升级，在提升生活品质需求的服务业发展过程中，切实把绿色发展理念贯穿于服务发展的始终。

加强专业性服务人才培养，提高创新支撑能力。服务业作为知识、人才高密集型产业，各类“高精尖”专业化人才是创新发展的重要基础，是服务业高质量发展的保障。创新是发展现代服务业的第一要素，通过创新产业结构、创新产业发展机制、创新制度政策、创新发展观念等提升服务业发展质量。黄河流域各省区结合产业发展需要、突出创新驱动、激发人才活力和优化服务保障进一步补齐政策短板，加大文化旅游、服务贸易、电子商务、会展营销等领域的人才培养力度，提高金融、信息技术、科学研究等领域的高层次人才比重，为现代服务业发展提供坚实保障。

转换传统动能，加快服务业战略性新兴产业发展速度。对于流域中上游地区，大力发展传统产业的同时，引进信息化技术，引导传统产业转型升级。黄河流域各省区优先发展交通运输网络配套物流设施和信息化平台，对设立战略性新兴产业创业投资引导基金等方式给予重点支持，加快发展金融业，培育新兴金融业态，创新金融产品，建设区域金融中心；推进大宗商品交易场所发展，鼓励发展总部经济和会展业，促进商务服务业快速发展。对于流域下游地区，积极培育现代医药、新一代信息技术和高端装备制造等新兴产业，利用区域交通优势和资源集聚

The training of professional service talents will be strengthened, and innovation support capabilities will be enhanced. As a knowledge and talent-intensive industry, the service sector relies heavily on various high-level and specialized experts for innovative development and high-quality growth. Innovation is the primary factor for developing the modern service industry, and the quality of service industry development can be enhanced through innovation in industrial structure, development mechanisms, institutional policies, and development concepts. The provinces and regions in the Yellow River Basin will further strengthen policy shortcomings, combining the needs of industrial development, emphasizing innovation drive, stimulating talent vitality, and optimizing service support to increase the training of talents in fields such as culture and tourism, service trade, e-commerce, and exhibition marketing. They will also increase the proportion of high-level experts in fields such as finance, information technology, and scientific research, providing solid guarantees for the development of the modern service industry.

Transform traditional momentum and accelerate the development of strategic emerging industries in the service sector. For the upper and middle reaches of the Yellow River Basin, while energetically developing traditional industries, information technology should be introduced to guide the transformation and modernization of traditional industries. Provinces and regions in the Yellow River Basin should give priority to the development of transportation and logistics facilities, as well as information platforms, and provide key support through the establishment of venture capital funds for strategic emerging industries. Efforts should be made to accelerate the development of the financial industry, cultivate emerging financial business models, innovate financial products, and establish regional financial centers. The development of commodity trading venues should be promoted, and the development of headquarters economy and exhibition industry should be encouraged to facilitate the rapid growth of the business service industry. For the lower portions of the river basin, modern pharmaceuticals, new-generation information technology, high-end equipment manufacturing, and other emerging industries should be actively cultivated. The advantages of regional transportation and resource aggregation should be utilized to promote the development of ecological tourism, commercial circulation, cultural and sports industries, and elderly care services in order to form new economic growth points.

优势，积极发展生态旅游、商贸流通、文化体育、健康养老等服务业，形成新的经济增长点。

以自主创新为引领，培育贸易竞争优势，优化贸易结构。创新驱动是贸易高质量发展的灵魂，是提升商品价值链的关键动力。加大财税政策力度，支持企业加大对关键“卡脖子”技术的研发投入，打造开放、高效、协同的技术研发平台，强化自主研发能力和企业综合创新能力，以新技术引导传统产业转型升级，全面创新产品、创新商业贸易模式，推进贸易与互联网、人工智能、区块链和大数据等深度融合。夯实贸易发展的产业基础。发展和培育新兴产业，加强生产性服务业和先进制造业的深度融合，打造具有竞争力和全球影响力的先进制造业集群；优化国际、国内市场布局和市场主体。增强与“一带一路”周边国家的贸易互助，扩大与“一带一路”周边国家贸易规模。及时把握黄河流域生态保护和高质量发展战略机遇，深入推进黄河流域内各省区间的联动发展。

以数字化赋能培养贸易新业态，加速转型升级。将生产性服务业推进到专业化和价值链高端延伸方向发展，即将数字化技术与研发设计、现代物流、现代先进农业、先进制造业等深度融合，加速推进生产性服务业数字化发展；推动生活性服务业向高品质和多样化升级，即将数字化赋能健康、养老、育幼、文化、旅游、体育、家政、物业等生活性服

Led by independent innovation, trade competitiveness should be cultivated, and trade structure should be optimized. Innovation-driven is the soul of high-quality trade development and the key driving force to improve the value chain of commodities. Financial and tax policies should be intensified to support enterprises in increasing research and development investment in key "bottleneck" technologies, creating open, efficient, and collaborative technology research and development platforms, and strengthening independent research and development capabilities and comprehensive innovation capabilities of enterprises. New technologies should be used to guide the transformation and upgrading of traditional industries, comprehensively innovate products and commercial trade models, and promote the deep integration of trade with the Internet, artificial intelligence, blockchain, big data, and other areas. The industrial foundation of trade development should be solidified. New emerging industries should be developed and nurtured, and the deep integration of productive service industries and advanced manufacturing industries should be strengthened to build advanced manufacturing clusters that are competitive and have global influence. The layout and main subjects in international and domestic markets should be optimized. Trade cooperation with countries along the "Belt and Road" should be strengthened, and the scale of trade with neighboring countries along the "Belt and Road" corridor should be expanded. The strategic opportunity for ecological protection and high-quality development in the Yellow River Basin should be timely grasped, and the coordinated development among provinces and regions in the Yellow River Basin should be promoted.

Cultivate new forms of trade by digitization and accelerate transformation and upgrading. The productive service industry is pushed towards specialization and high-end value chain extension by integrating digital technology with research and development, design, modern logistics, advanced agriculture, and advanced manufacturing, thus accelerating the digital development of the productive service industry. The quality and diversity of the consumer service industry are upgraded by digitization, which enhances the level of digital intelligence in public service through empowering health care, elderly care, child care, culture, tourism, sports, home economics, and property management. With data-driven strategies at the core, trade as the leading factor, industries as the mainstay, platforms as the foundation, and data as the driving force, promote the

务业，提高公共服务数字化智能发展程度。以数据驱动为核心、以贸易为龙头、以产业为主体、以平台为支撑，推进贸易实现数字化和智能化管理，提升外贸服务综合数字化水平，推进产业数字化和数字产业化发展，打造具有国际竞争力的数字化产业集群。对于跨境电子商务综合试验区建设的成熟做法积极推广，完善管理体制和政策措施，建立数据资源产权、跨境传输和交易流通等标准规范，推动信息共享和联合监管。

以黄河文化为主线，打造黄河流域中华文化长廊，构建黄河文化贸易格局。以黄河为轴线，加大黄河流域文化投入，结合流域历史文化、水文化特色和生态条件；考虑黄河流域生态环境、旅游开发和文化传承等要素，以生态环境保护为基础，实现黄河流域生态系统、文化系统和旅游系统的有机融合。各区域应结合自身历史积淀和文化底蕴等优势内生动力，根据本地的资源特点与经济发展状况进行功能定位，着力打造黄河生态环境保护、文化旅游等领域的黄河样板，促进黄河流域文化旅游产业蓬勃发展。大力推进建设黄河流域文化出口基地，培育发展特色文创产业，深入挖掘黄河流域特色文化资源，全力做好“文化贸易”“文化制造”等创新性发展，推进文化资源向文化产业转化。同时，借助“一带一路”等国家战略传播黄河优秀文化，带动更多中国文化、产品和服务走出去，构建黄河文化贸易格局。

digitalization and intelligent management of trade, enhance the comprehensive digitalization level of foreign trade services, drive the industrial digitalization and the development of digital industries, and build digital industrial clusters with international competitiveness. Mature practices in the construction of comprehensive experimental zones for cross-border e-commerce are actively promoted, the management system and policies are improved, and standard specifications for data resource property rights, cross-border transmission, and transaction circulation are established to promote information sharing and joint-supervision.

Taking the Yellow River culture as the guidance, a long corridor of Chinese culture in the Yellow River Basin is being built,and the Yellow River cultural trade pattern is constructed. Along the axis of the Yellow River, cultural investment in the Yellow River Basin is increased, combining the historical and cultural characteristics and ecological conditions of the basin. Based on ecological environment protection, the organic integration of the ecological system of the Yellow River Basin, cultural system, and tourism system is achieved, considering the factors such as ecological environment, tourism development, and cultural heritage of the Yellow River Basin. Each region should combine its own historical accumulation and cultural heritage with its advantages and economic development status to establish functional positioning, focusing on creating a template of the Yellow River in the areas of ecological environment protection and cultural tourism to promote the flourishing development of the cultural tourism industry in the Yellow River Basin. Great efforts are made to promote the construction of the Yellow River Basin cultural export base, cultivate and develop distinctive cultural and creative industries, deeply tap into the unique cultural resources of the Yellow River Basin, and encourage and create an innovative way of life in "cultural trade" and "cultural manufacturing", promoting the transformation of cultural resources into cultural industries. At the same time, with the help of national strategies such as the Belt and Road Initiative, the outstanding culture of the Yellow River is destined to drive more Chinese culture, products, and services to go abroad, constructing a Yellow River cultural trade pattern.

With green circular development as the core, the optimization of industrial structure and exploration of new industrial development models are being pursued

以绿色循环为核心，优化产业结构，探寻产业发展新模式。科学调控黄河流域范围内大中型城市规模，以城市群为发展中心，稳步推进宁夏沿黄城市群、关中平原城市群、兰西城市群、呼包鄂榆城市群、晋中城市群、中原城市群和山东半岛城市群的产业发展，利用城市群内的资源特色，形成优势互补的产业发展结构，上游城市群产业发展要着重强化生态保护、水源涵养功能，创造更多生态产品。中游城市群产业发展要利用好煤炭资源，严格控制污染处理，促进产业园内污染处理设施的统一建设。下游地区城市群产业发展则应向新兴产业方向发展，同时要推广集约节水模式；对外商业贸易中，大力发展绿色贸易，严格控制高污染、高耗能产品，激励企业构建绿色技术支撑体系和供应链，开展绿色设计和绿色制造，采用国际先进环保标准，取得低碳、节能绿色产品认证资格，实现企业、产业可持续发展。

综上，“十三五”期间，黄河流域服务业得以持续、高速发展，所占比重也持续提升，互联网技术、高科技以及金融手段等数字经济的发展有效支撑了流域服务业的多层次发展。

在“十四五”发展过程，黄河流域正逐步在绿色循环发展、打造服务业多业态、数字化赋能等多方面深化服务业高质量发展。旨在“十四五”期间，打造形成黄河流域生产性服务业中心，大力推动现代金融、物流、科技服务、商贸等多模块的交叉互融，强化先进制造与生产性服务的相互促进发展。打造黄河流域生活性服务业品牌，形成基于黄河文化、自然资源为符号特色的服务业产品。

in the Yellow River Basin. The large and medium-sized cities in the Yellow River Basin are being scientifically regulated, with urban clusters as the development center. The industrial development of the Ningxia-Yellow River urban cluster, Guanzhong Plain urban cluster, Lanxi urban cluster, Hubei Plain urban cluster, Jinzhong urban cluster, Central Plains urban cluster, and Shandong Peninsula urban cluster is being steadily promoted. The characteristic resources within the urban clusters are being utilized to form a complementary industrial development structure. The upstream urban clusters should focus on strengthening ecological protection and water conservation functions to create more ecological products. The midstream urban clusters should make good use of coal resources, strictly control pollution treatment, and promote the unified construction of pollution treatment facilities within industrial parks. The downstream urban clusters should develop towards emerging industries and promote intensive water-saving models. In foreign trade, green trade should be vigorously developed while strictly controlling highly-polluting and high-energy-consuming products. Enterprises should be encouraged to build a green technology support system and supply chain, carry out sustainable design and manufacturing, adopt international advanced environmental standards, obtain low-carbon, energy-saving, and green product certification qualifications, and achieve an environmentally friendly development of both enterprises and industries.

In summary, during the 13th Five-Year Plan period, the service industry in the Yellow River Basin has continued to develop rapidly, with its market share continuously increasing. The development of digital economy, such as internet technology, high-tech, and financial means, has effectively supported the multi-level development of the service industry.

During the 14th Five-Year Plan period, the Yellow River Basin is gradually deepening the high-quality development of the service industry in various aspects such as green circular development, the creation of multiple service industry, and digital empowerment. We will build a producer service center, vigorously promote the cross-integration of modern finance, logistics, sci-tech services, and trade, and strengthen the mutual promotion and development of advanced manufacturing and producer services. We will also build brand advantage in consumer services in the Yellow River Basin, and provide services characterized by the Yellow River culture and natural resources.

第四章

城市和城市群高质量发展

Chapter 4

High-quality Development of Cities and City Clusters

2016年，中国城镇化率已经达到57%，有近8亿城镇人口，约为世界城镇人口的1/5，亚太地区城镇人口的3/5。近年来，中国基本保持着城镇化率每年增长1个百分点的发展速度，城镇化发展进入高速增长的中后期。中心城市是所在城市群的区域中心，中心城市在城市群层面应体现对城市群内其他大中小城市的引领、带动作用。

中心城市和城市群是经济发展要素的重要载体，对区域协同发展、培育新型增长极具有主导作用。中心城市发挥其带动引领作用，落实好黄河流域生态保护和高质量发展这一重大国家战略，提升黄河流域综合承载力和资源配置效率，形成优势互补、高质量发展的区域经济布局，推动黄河流域生态保护和高质量发展。

一、城市与产业发展

发挥中心城市辐射带动作用有助于增强黄河流域区域间经济联系。中心城市作为核心引领区，通过对周边地区的要素资源的吸收来弥补自身短板，同时通过集聚效应为周边地区提供技术、人才、资金等资源。在中心城市的影响下，周边地区积极提供配套服务，发展相关产业，推动了全方位的发展，扩大了经济腹地的规模。黄河流域正在逐步推进兰州－西宁城市群的发展，强化黄河“几”字弯都市圈的协同发展，深化西安、郑州国家中心城市的带动作用，发挥山东半岛城市群的领导作用，推动沿黄地区中心城市及城市群实现高质量发展。

1. 黄河流域中心城市——郑州高质量发展优势

郑州市文化底蕴深厚，人文气息浓重，具有丰富的黄河文化、商都文化、拜祖文化及戏曲文化等，拥有较强的核心区位优势，为其高质量发展奠定了良好的基础。

郑州作为河南省会，总面积7567平方千米，2022年年底常住人口1300.8万人，地区生产总值12934.7亿元。郑州市常住总人口数从2012

In 2016, China's urbanization rate had reached 57%, with nearly 800 million urban residents, accounting for about one-fifth of the world's urban population and three-fifths of the urban population in the Asia-Pacific region. In recent years, China has basically maintained an annual increase of one percent in the urbanization rate, and the development of urbanization has entered the mid-to-late stage of rapid growth. As the regional hub of its urban cluster, a central city should demonstrate its leading and driving role over other large, medium, and small cities within the city cluster.

Central cities and city clusters are important carriers of economic development and play a leading role in promoting regional collaborative development and fostering new growth poles. Central cities leverage their driving and leading roles to effectively implement the significant national strategy of ecological protection and high-quality development, enhance the comprehensive carrying capacity and resource allocation efficiency, form a regional economic layout with complementary advantages and high-quality development, and promote ecological protection and high-quality development in the Yellow River Basin region.

I. Urban Development and Industrial Growth

Leveraging the radiating and driving effect of central cities helps to strengthen economic ties among different areas in the Yellow River Basin region. As the core leading area, a central city compensates for their own shortcomings by absorbing resource elements from surrounding areas, while also providing surrounding areas with resources such as technologies, talents, and fundings through agglomeration effects. Under the influence of the central city, surrounding areas actively provide supporting services and develop related industries, promoting comprehensive development and expanding the scale of the economic hinterland. The Yellow River Basin region is gradually advancing the development of the Lanzhou-Xining city cluster, strengthening the collaborative development of the metropolitan circle in the "几"-shaped bend of the Yellow River, deepening the driving effect of Xi'an and Zhengzhou as national central cities, and leveraging the leadership of the Shandong Peninsula city cluster to promote high-

郑州市郑东新区鸟瞰图

Bird's Eye View of Zhengdong New District in Zhengzhou

年的948万增加到2022年的1300.8万，10年净流入300多万人口，城市吸引力持续提升，“城市年轻力指数”全国第五，上榜“全国十大最多人口净流入城市”，这也为未来发展提供了充足的劳动力。同时，作为全国的交通枢纽，郑州也被称为“火车拉来的城市”。郑州作为全国重要综合交通枢纽和现代物流中心，拥有公路、铁路与航空货运交通优势，成为中部城市物流集散地。其中，以郑州为中心，形成“双十字”铁路客运枢纽和“米”字形高铁网。2022年6月20日，济郑高铁濮阳至郑州段、郑渝高铁以及郑州航空港站“携手”开通运营，标志着河南省建成以郑州为核心的“米”字形高铁网，并实现17个省辖市全部通高铁。至此，河南省铁路运营里程达到6716公里，其中时速350公里的高速铁路里程达到1924公里，居全国第1位。2022年，在中国权威媒体《第一财经报》发布的中国338个地级以上城市商业魅力排名，郑

quality development of central cities and city clusters along the Yellow River.

1. Zhengzhou, a Central City in the Yellow River Basin Region with High-Quality Development

Zhengzhou has a profound cultural heritage and a strong humanistic atmosphere, with a rich array of Yellow River culture, Shang Dynasty capital culture, ancestral veneration culture, and traditional opera culture. It also possesses a strong core geographical advantage, which has laid a solid foundation for its high-quality development.

Zhengzhou, as the capital city of Henan Province, covers a total area of 7,567 square kilometers with a permanent population of 13.008 million people by the end of 2022 and a regional gross domestic product of 1,293.47 billion yuan. The total permanent population of Zhengzhou increased from 9.48 million in 2012 to 13.008 million in 2022, with a net inflow of more than 3 million people for 10 years. The city's attractiveness continues to rise, ranking fifth in the national "Urban Youthfulness Index" and making it onto the list of the "Top Ten Cities with the Largest Population Inflow in China", which also provides a sufficient labor force for future development. At the same time, as a national transportation hub, Zhengzhou is also known as the "city brought by the train". Zhengzhou, serving as a crucial comprehensive transportation hub and modern logistics center in the country, boasts advantages in road, rail, and air freight transportation, making it a logistics hub for central cities. Centered around Zhengzhou, a "double-cross" railway passenger hub and a "米" (Mi, a Chinese character)-shaped high-speed rail network have been established. On June 20, 2022, the Puyang-Zhengzhou section of the Jining-Zhengzhou high-speed railway, the Zhengzhou-Chongqing high-speed railway, and the Zhengzhou Airport Railway Station were jointly put into operation, marking the completion of the "米"-shaped high-speed railway network in Henan Province with Zhengzhou as the core center, and achieving high-speed rail access to all 17 provincial cities under its jurisdiction. To date, Henan's railway operation mileage has reached 6,716 kilometers, with 1,924 kilometers of high-speed rail operating at a speed of 350 kilometers per hour, ranking first in the nation. According to the authoritative media outlet *China Business News*, in 2022, Zhengzhou was listed as a "new first-tier city" in the ranking of commercial attractiveness among 338 cities at or above prefecture

州市入选“新一线城市”名单，为黄河流域的城市群建设发挥着中心城市的引领作用。

2. 黄河流域中心城市——西安高质量发展优势

西安位于我国中西部重要经济区的交界处，是国家“一带一路”倡议和西部大开发战略的重点区域，国家重要的科研、教育、工业基地。西安总面积约 10108 平方千米，2022 年年底常住人口 1299.59 万人，城镇人口 1034.34 万人，城镇化率 79.59%。作为西北至西南、中原、华东和华北地区的交通枢纽，它在古代中外经济文化交往中是重要的中心区位。同时，它拥有我国最大的国际内陆港——西安国际港务区，在我国经济发展中具有承东启西、连接南北的区位优势。

西安北站作为亚洲较大的高铁枢纽，是陕西省交通网络的重要组成部分。它连接了 6 条国家高速公路，使得陕西省构建了由高速铁路

西安市鸟瞰图（夜景）

Bird's Eye View of Night Scene of Xi'an

level in China. As a central city, Zhengzhou plays a leading role in the city cluster development of the Yellow River Basin region.

2. Xi'an—a Central City of the Yellow River Basin Region with High-Quality Development

Xi'an is located at the intersection of China's important economic regions in the central and western parts, and is a key area for the national "Belt and Road" initiative and the Western Development Strategy, as well as an important base for scientific research, education, and industry. Xi'an covers an area of about 10,108 square kilometers, and by the end of 2022 the permanent resident population has reached 12.9959 million, and the urban population 10.3434 million, with an urbanization rate at 79.59%. As a transportation hub from the northwest to the southwest, Central Plains, East China, and North China, it occupies an important central position in ancient economic and cultural exchanges between China and countries overseas. At the same time, it has the largest international inland port in China—the Xi'an International Port Area, which plays a pivotal role in our country's economic development by connecting the east with the west and linking the north with the south.

Xi'an North Station, as a relatively larger high-speed railway hub in Asia, is an important part of Shaanxi Province's transportation network. It connects six national expressways, enabling Shanxi Province to build a integrated transportation hub comprising high-speed railway networks, highways and airports, which provides strong momentum for the high-quality development and regional integration in Shanxi Province. At the same time, Xi'an is gradually building a land, air, and sea intermodal transport channel, forming a three-dimensional seamless large logistics system, which further accelerates Xi'an's integration into the global economy. The rapid development and quality improvement of the logistics industry can not only promote resources flow but also inject new momentum and vitality into Xi'an's development, whereas narrowing the development gap between inland and coastal areas. With the deepening development of Xi'an's hub economy, the agglomeration effect of the logistics industry on the industry is becoming increasingly prominent, attracting more and more high-end resources to gather in Xi'an, providing momentum for the collaborative development of major regional industries. Xi'an's logistics

网、公路网和航空港组成的综合交通枢纽，为陕西省的高质量发展和区域融合发展提供了强大的动力。同时，西安正在逐步建设陆空海联运通道，形成了立体无缝的大物流体系，进一步加速了西安融入全球经济的步伐。物流业的快速发展和提质增效不仅能够促进要素流动，还能为西安的发展注入新的动力和活力，同时也缩小了内陆与沿海地区的发展差距。随着西安枢纽经济的深化发展，物流业对产业的集聚效应不断凸显，吸引了越来越多的高端资源在西安集聚，为区域重大产业的协同发展提供了动力。西安的物流业不仅仅是连接着各类运输工具的纽带，更是区域经济发展的重要支撑。

西安作为中国历史上历经朝代最多、影响力最大的城市，拥有独特的历史条件。这使得西安的独特魅力在全国得到充分释放，不仅促进了当地旅游业和手工业的发展，还推动了国际旅游枢纽的建设与发展。

3. 黄河流域中心城市——济南高质量发展优势

济南是中华文明的重要发祥地之一，承载着齐鲁文化和儒家文化的传承与弘扬。这里融合了龙山文化、泉水文化、诗词文化等多种特色文化，拥有 30 处全国重点文物保护单位，如城子崖遗址、齐长城遗址等。济南还是中国非物质文化遗产博览会永久落户地，拥有丰富的非遗资源，如黄河号子、黄河大秧歌等，展现了黄河文化的多样性。

济南总面积 10244.45 平方千米，2022 年年底常住人口 941.5 万，城镇人口 699.8 万，城镇化率 74.3%，2022 年，济南全市地区生产总值达到 12027.5 亿元，市场主体数量超过 140 万户，规模以上企业突破 1 万家，上市企业达到 50 家，落户济南的世界 500 强企业、央企数量迅速攀升，在全国营商环境便利度评价中位居第 7，在“2022 年中国百强城市排行榜”中排名第 14 位。济南拥有得天独厚的区位优势，北接京津冀、南连长三角、东承环渤海经济圈、西通中原经济区，高铁网络覆盖 4.1 亿人口，形成 1.5 小时高铁圈。其高铁直达城市数量仅次于北京，路网“三环十二射”高快一体，交通便捷。作为京沪高铁 5 大枢纽

industry is not only the link connecting various transportation tools but also an important support for regional economic development.

Xi'an, as the city that has experienced most ancient dynasties and held the greatest influence in Chinese history, enjoys unique historical advantages. This has allowed Xi'an's unique charm to be fully released nationwide, promoting not only the development of local tourism and handicrafts but also the construction and development of an international tourism hub.

3. Jinan—a Central City of the Yellow River Basin Region with High-Quality Development

Jinan is one of the important cradles of Chinese civilization, bearing the legacy and inheritance of Qilu (mainly Shandong Province) and Confucian culture. It integrates various distinctive cultures, such as Longshan culture, spring culture, and poetry culture, and has 30 major cultural heritage sites under national-level protection, such as the Chengzi Cliff site and the Qi Great Wall site. Jinan is also the permanent host city of the China Intangible Cultural Heritage Expo, boasting rich intangible cultural heritage resources such as the Yellow River folk songs and the Yellow River Da Yangge dance, showcasing the diversity of Yellow River culture.

Jinan has a total area of 10,244.45 square kilometers. By the end of 2022, its permanent resident population is 9.415 million, and its urban population 6.998 million, with an urbanization rate at 74.3%. In 2022, the total regional GDP of Jinan reached 1,202.75 billion yuan, with the number of market entities exceeding 1.4 million, over 10,000 large-scale enterprises, 50 listed companies, and the number of Fortune Global 500 and Chinese central State-owned enterprises settled in Jinan rapidly increasing. It ranks 7th in the national business environment convenience evaluation and 14th in the "2022 China Top 100 Cities". Jinan has a unique location advantage, connecting the Beijing-Tianjin-Hebei to the north, the Yangtze River Delta to the south, the Bohai Rim Economic Circle to the east, and the Central Plains Economic Zone to the west. The high-speed rail network, forming a 1.5-hour high-speed rail circle, benefits 410 million people. Its number of cities directly reached by high-speed rail ranks second only after Beijing, with a road network of "three rings and twelve radii". Jinan has a comprehensive and three-dimensional transportation system, as one of

黄河济南段沿岸的绿色生态景观带（新华社）
Green Ecological Landscape Belt Along Jinan Section of the Yellow River (Xinhua News Agency)

之一，以及全国 45 个公路主枢纽和 21 个物流节点城市之一，济南拥有完善的综合立体交通体系。济南新旧动能转换起步区是继雄安新区起步区之后的第二个起步区。它的使命在于成为黄河流域生态保护和高质量发展的新典范，充分体现黄河重大国家战略的实施成效。起步区正在迅速崛起，逐步展现出“黄河流域最具现代化特色的璀璨明珠”，将充分发挥“流域标杆”作用。济南新旧动能转换起步区的成效，将为沿黄城市在“黄河文章”和高质量发展方面提供宝贵经验，为实施黄河重大国家战略做出重要贡献。山东是面向日韩和东盟的“桥头堡”，黄河流域

the five major hubs of the Beijing-Shanghai high-speed railway, and one of the 45 main highway hubs in China and 21 logistics node cities. The Jinan New and Old Energy Conversion Pilot Area is the second pilot area ranking only after the Xiong'an New Area. Its mission is to become a new model of ecological protection and high-quality development in the Yellow River Basin region, fully reflecting the implementation effect of the major national strategy of the Yellow River. The pilot area is rapidly rising and gradually showing "the brightest pearl with the most modern characteristics in the Yellow River Basin region", which will give full play to the "benchmark" role of the basin region. The effectiveness of the Jinan New and Old Energy Conversion Pilot Area will provide valuable experience for cities along the Yellow River in the "Yellow River Scope" and high-quality development, making an important contribution to the implementation of the major national strategy of the Yellow River. Shandong is a "bridgehead" facing Japan, South Korea, and ASEAN, the only river-sea intersection area and the only province in the Yellow River Basin region with both land and sea resources, which has a strong economic complementarity and high resource matching with other provinces and regions along the Yellow River Basin region. As the most convenient "outlet" along the Yellow River Basin region, Shandong Port bears an important responsibility and mission in fully integrating into and serving the ecological protection and high-quality development of the Yellow River Basin region. As the core of the Shandong Peninsula city cluster, Jinan is the leader in ecological protection and high-quality development of the Yellow River Basin region. Its leading role is crucial for giving full play to the leading role of the Shandong Peninsula city cluster and at the same time, Jinan has an important impact on the high-quality development of the entire Yellow River Basin region and the smooth implementation of the national regional coordinated development strategy.

4. Qingdao—A Key Opening-up Gateway of the Yellow River Basin Region with High-Quality Development

Qingdao is located in the eastern coastal area of China, adjacent to

唯一河海交汇区，沿黄流域唯一“陆海兼具”的省份，与沿黄流域其他省区经济互补性强、资源匹配度高。作为沿黄流域最便捷的“出海口”，山东港口在全面融入和服务黄河流域生态保护和高质量发展方面肩负着重要的责任和使命。济南作为山东半岛城市群的核心，是黄河流域生态保护和高质量发展的领头羊。济南的龙头作用对于发挥山东半岛城市群的引领作用至关重要，同时对整个黄河流域的高质量发展和国家区域协调发展战略的顺利实施产生重要影响。

4. 黄河流域重要开放门户——青岛高质量发展优势

青岛位于中国东部沿海地区，毗邻黄海、渤海，与日本、韩国隔海相望，是我国重要的海上贸易门户。尽管黄河不流经青岛，但青岛却是黄河流域最主要的经济出海口，拥有天然的“东西双向互济、陆海内外联动”优势，对于促进市场资源要素的加速流动、循环和联通具有独特的枢纽作用。青岛港承载了沿黄地区大量商品的装船出口，连接着全球市场；同时，来自世界各地的货物也源源不断地输送至青岛港。截至2022年底，青岛港已经规划建设了31个内陆港，其中涵盖了沿黄九省区的27个内陆港，海铁联运班列数量已增至70条，其中沿黄九省区的班列数量达到60条。2022年仅青岛港的货物吞吐量就达到了6.6亿吨，其中涉及沿黄九省区的货物达到了5.4亿吨。青岛拥有得天独厚的地理条件，拥有着金沙滩、琅琊台、崂山、董家口港等优质资源，依托大山东的各类基础支撑，面向广袤的太平洋，足以担当黄河流域的天然出海大通道、联通世界的关键“节点”，被中央赋予在黄河流域生态保护和高质量发展中提升核心城市竞争力、发挥港口门户城市优势的国之重任。

the Yellow Sea and the Bohai Sea, facing Japan and South Korea across the sea, and is an important maritime trade gateway for our country. Although the Yellow River does not flow through Qingdao, it is the main economic outlet of the Yellow River Basin region, with a natural advantage of "mutual aid between the east and west, and linkage of land, sea, and overseas", playing a unique role in promoting the accelerated flow, circulation, and connection of market resources. Qingdao Port undertakes a large amount of commodity loading and export along the Yellow River area, connecting to the global market; at the same time, goods from all over the world are also continuously transported to Qingdao Port. By the end of 2022, Qingdao Port had planned and constructed 31 inland ports, including 27 inland ports in the nine provinces and regions along the Yellow River, and the number of sea-rail intermodal train lines has increased to 70, of which the number of train lines in the nine provinces and regions along the Yellow River has reached 60. In 2022, the cargo throughput of Qingdao Port reached 660 million tons, of which the cargo involving the nine provinces and regions along the Yellow River reached 540 million tons. Qingdao has unique geographical conditions, with high-quality resources such as Jinsha Beach, Langyatai, Laoshan, and Dongjiakou Port. With the support of various foundations in Shandong Province and facing the vast Pacific Ocean, Qingdao is capable of serving as a natural gateway to the sea in the Yellow River Basin region and a key "node" connecting the world. It is entrusted by the central government with the important task of enhancing the competitiveness of core cities and leveraging the advantages of port gateway cities in ecological protection and high-quality development of the Yellow River Basin region.

Ranking among the megacities, Qingdao covers a total area of 11,293 square kilometers, with a permanent resident population of 10.3421 million by the end of 2022, an urbanization rate at 77.32%. In 2022, the total regional GDP of Qingdao City reached 1,492.08 billion yuan, making it the economic leader of the Yellow River Basin region, which is inseparable from Qingdao's excellent ability to open up to the outside world. According to the Qingdao Customs statistics, in 2021, the total value of Qingdao's foreign trade import and export was 849.84 billion yuan, setting a new historical high for the fifth consecutive year since 2017, and the growth rate ranked fifth among the 15 sub-provincial

青岛港前湾QQCT集装箱码头(新华社记者李紫恒摄)
Qianwan QQCT Container Pier of Qingdao Port (Photographed by Li Ziheng, Xinhua News Agency)

青岛总面积 11293 平方千米，2022 年年底常住人口 1034.21 万人，跻身特大城市行列，城镇化率 77.32%，2022 年青岛全市地区生产总值达到 14920.8 亿元，是黄河流域的经济第一城，这离不开青岛卓越的对外开放能力。据青岛海关统计，2021 年青岛市外贸进出口总值 8498.4 亿元人民币，自 2017 年以来连续第 5 年刷新历史新高，在全国 15 个副省级城市中，增速位居第五位。青岛市的地理环境优越，远离大型山脉，濒临海洋，土地平坦，发展空间大。青岛市的区位优势明显，这里是环渤海经济圈和山东半岛蓝色经济区的核心城市，同时也是中日韩自贸区的前沿地带，更是“一带一路”经济走廊主要节点城市。青岛市的交通运输发达。机场方面，在运营的有青岛流亭国际机场，在建的有青岛胶东国际机场。铁路方面有青岛站、青岛北站。青岛市也是国际性港口城市，青岛港地处国际主航线的必经之路，向内就是环渤海经济圈和长江三角洲经济区，青岛港是中国第二个外贸亿吨吞吐大港，全球第六大港口，国际集装箱航线总数稳居中国北方港口之首。空港方面，即将

cities in the country. Qingdao, far from large mountain ranges, bordering the sea, boasts a superior geographical environment, with flat land and ample space for development. Qingdao's location advantage is evident; it is a core city in the Bohai Rim Economic Circle and the Shandong Peninsula Blue Economic Zone, a frontier city of the China-Japan-Korea Free Trade Area, and a major node city in the Belt and Road Economic Corridor. Qingdao's transportation is well-developed. In terms of airports, there is Qingdao Liuting International Airport at operation and Qingdao Jiaodong International Airport under-construction. For railways, there are Qingdao Station and Qingdao North Station. Qingdao is also an international port city. Qingdao Port is on the main international shipping route, with the Bohai Rim Economic Circle and the Yangtze River Delta Economic Zone to its interior. Qingdao Port is the second-largest foreign trade port in China in terms of tonnage, the sixth-largest port globally, and its total number of international container shipping routes is consistently at the top among the northern ports of China. In terms of air transportation, the soon-to-be-operated Jiaodong International Airport is a 4F-level airport, which directly enhances Qingdao's "air strength", with two planned 3,600-meter long-range runways capable of accommodating the world's largest aircraft models such as the Airbus A380 and Boeing 787. In the "National 14th Five-Year Plan for Port Development", Qingdao is listed as one of the four major ports in the Bohai Rim area; in the layout of air ports, Qingdao becomes one of the 29 regional hubs in the country. In the earlier "National Comprehensive Transportation Network Plan Outline", Qingdao was included in the list of 20 cities to accelerate the construction of international comprehensive transportation hubs and was positioned as an "international comprehensive transportation hub city".

Relying on Qingdao's unique location and excellent opening-up capabilities, it effectively compensates for the deficiencies in the Yellow River Basin region's external opening-up capabilities, building the most convenient outlet to the sea in the Yellow River Basin region. Qingdao, aiming to build itself as an international gateway hub city, plays the role of "economic outlet" and open portal of the Yellow River Basin region, and is deeply implementing the regional coordinated development strategy. It further enhances its open radiation capacity to the Yellow River Basin region and shares the opportunities for open development.

转场运营的胶东国际机场为4F级，直接拉升青岛的“空中实力”，规划建设的两条3600米远距跑道，可起降空客A380、波音787等世界最大机型。在《国家“十四五”口岸发展规划》中，青岛被列为环渤海4大主要口岸之一；在航空口岸布局中，青岛成为全国29个区域枢纽之一。在更早之前的《国家综合立体交通网规划纲要》中，青岛进入20个加快建设的国际性综合交通枢纽城市名单，被定位为“国际性综合交通枢纽城市”。

依托于青岛的独特区位和卓越的开放能力，有效地弥补了黄河流域对外开放能力的不足和缺陷，构筑了黄河流域最便捷的出海通道，锚定打造国际门户枢纽城市的青岛，发挥黄河流域“经济出海口”和开放门户作用，正在深入实施区域协调发展战略，向黄河流域进一步增强开放辐射能力，共享开放发展机遇。

二、城市建设协同发展

黄河流域上游至下游共包含7个城市群，面积约85.74万平方公里，占黄河流域9省区的24.01%。黄河流域7个城市群拥有较高的人口集中度，其经济指标也在黄河9省区中占有较大比重，是黄河流域高质量发展的重要支柱。其中包括：以兰州和西宁为双中心的兰西城市群、以银川为中心的宁夏沿黄城市群、以呼和浩特为中心的呼包鄂榆城市群、以西安为中心的关中平原城市群、以太原为中心的晋中城市群、以郑州为中心的中原城市群、以济南和青岛为双中心的山东半岛城市群。

通过黄河流域城市群点上的高质量发展带动黄河流域全域面上的高水平保护，不断增强黄河流域城市群的辐射作用，是黄河战略的重要举措。相对而言，沿黄城市群具有产业基础好、人口容纳能力强的特征，是流域内要素配置和要素集聚能力相对较强的区域，这是优势产业集聚、集群和集约发展的有利条件。

II. Urban Construction and Collaborative Development

The Yellow River Basin region, from upstream to downstream, includes 7 city clusters, covering an area of about 857,400 square kilometers, accounting for 24.01% of the nine provinces and regions in the Yellow River Basin region. The seven city clusters in the Yellow River Basin region have a high population concentration, and their economic indicators hold a significant proportion in the nine provinces and regions, making them an important pillar for the high-quality development of the Yellow River Basin region. This includes the Lanxi city cluster with Lanzhou and Xining as the dual centers, the Ningxia Yellow River Basin region city cluster with Yinchuan as the center, Hohhot-Baotou-Ordos-Yulin city cluster with Hohhot as the center, the Guanzhong Plains city cluster with Xi'an as the center, the Jinzhong city cluster with Taiyuan as the center, the Central Plains city cluster with Zhengzhou as the center, and the Shandong Peninsula city cluster with Jinan and Qingdao as the dual centers.

By promoting high-quality development in the city clusters along the Yellow River, it drives a high level of protection across the entire basin of the Yellow River. Continuously enhancing the radiating effect of the city clusters in the Yellow River Basin region is an important measure of the Yellow River Strategy. Comparatively, the city clusters along the Yellow River have good industrial foundations and strong population capacity, making them relatively strong areas in terms of resources allocation and agglomeration within the Yellow River Basin. This provides favorable conditions for the agglomeration, clustering, and intensive development of advantageous industries.

1.Lanzhou-Xining City Cluster

The Lanzhou-Xining city cluster is located in the southwestern part of the Yellow River Basin region, composed of parts of eastern Qinghai and southern Gansu. It holds the second most strategic position in China's northwest region after the Guanzhong Plain city cluster. The Lanzhou-Xining city cluster is rich in energy resources, with a significant proportion of the secondary industry in its economic structure, exceeding the national average. Under the major strategy of high-quality development, the Lanzhou-Xining city cluster is focusing on promoting the transformation and upgrading of traditional industries and vigorously developing the characteristic tourism industry to promote sustainable

1. 兰西城市群

兰西城市群位于黄河流域西南部，由青海东部和甘肃南部的部分地区组成，在我国西北地区战略地位仅次于关中平原城市群。兰西城市群能源资源丰富，经济结构中第二产业比重较大，其比重高于全国平均水平。在高质量发展重大战略下，兰西城市群着力推动传统产业转型升级，大力发展特色旅游产业，推动该区域的可持续发展。在生态保护方面，兰西城市群内部城市正探索以空间规划作为黄河生态保护的突破点，同时以三江源、祁连山、甘南黄河上游水源涵养区等为重点，推进实施一批重大生态保护修复和建设工程，提升水源涵养能力。

2. 宁夏沿黄城市群

宁夏沿黄城市群主要位于沃野千里的宁夏平原，东侧自南向北流动的黄河为农业发展提供了水源，成为西北地区为数不多的灌溉农业分布区。此外，宁夏沿黄城市群当前虽以第二产业为主发展经济，但正在加速传统优势产业转型升级步伐，发展绿色清洁能源，走能源转型发展之路，以特色旅游业为抓手发展第三产业，实现区域高质量发展。

3. 呼包鄂榆城市群

呼包鄂榆城市群主要包括内蒙古的呼和浩特市、鄂尔多斯市、包头市和陕西的榆林市等城市，面积达17.5万平方千米。资源富集，经济和科技文化相对发达，其生态地位、经济地位和战略地位十分重要。该城市群聚集众多自然景观，是黄河流域重要的生态屏障；布局大量工业园

development in the region. In terms of ecological protection, cities within the Lanzhou-Xining city cluster are exploring spatial planning as a breakthrough for the ecological protection of the Yellow River. They are focusing on key areas such as the San Jiang Yuan (Three Rivers Source), Qilian Mountains, and the water conservation areas in the upper reaches of the Yellow River in Gannan. The goal is to promote and implement a series of major ecological protection, restoration, and construction projects to enhance water conservation capacity.

2. Ningxia Yellow River Basin Region City Cluster

The Ningxia Yellow River Basin region city cluster is mainly located in the vast Ningxia Plain, where the Yellow River flows from south to north on the east side, providing water sources for agricultural development and becoming one of the few areas with irrigated agriculture in the northwest region. In addition, although the Ningxia Yellow River Basin region city cluster is currently developing its economy mainly through the secondary industry, it is accelerating the transformation and upgrading of traditional advantage industries, developing green and clean energy, and following the path of energy transformation and development. It is using the characteristic tourism industry as a starting point to develop the tertiary industry and achieve high-quality regional development.

3. Hohhot-Baotou-Ordos-Yulin City Cluster

The Hohhot-Baotou-Ordos-Yulin city cluster mainly includes cities such as Hohhot, Baotou, Ordos in Inner Mongolia, and Yulin in Shaanxi, covering an area of 175,000 square kilometers. It is rich in resources, relatively developed in economy, science, and culture, and holds a very important ecological, economic, and strategic position. This city cluster gathers many natural landscapes and is an important ecological barrier in the Yellow River Basin region; it has a large number of industrial parks, including industries such as energy, chemical, metallurgy, and building materials. It is located in the core area of the northern opening zone, the Yellow River economic belt, and the ecological protection zone. Also, it is a core area for the Belt and Road Initiative development, the China-Russia-Mongolia Economic Corridor, and the construction of the ecological barrier in the northern region of our country.

4. Guanzhong Plain City Cluster

The Guanzhong Plain city cluster spans three provinces of Shaanxi, Shanxi,

区，包括能源、化工、冶金、建材等产业；处在向北开放区、沿黄经济带和生态保护带的核心地带，是“一带一路”倡议、中俄蒙经济走廊、我国北方地区生态屏障建设的核心区域。

4. 关中平原城市群

关中平原城市群跨越陕西、山西、甘肃三省，包括11个市，连接黄河上中游，具有重要的经济联动发展和战略地位。关中平原城市群发展基础好、发展潜力大，在现代化建设大局和全方位开放格局中占据独特的战略地位。关中平原城市群是传统能源开发的重点区域、全国重要的装备制造业基地和高新技术产业基地，制造业发展迅猛，同时也是始祖文化和汉唐文化的发源地和兴盛地，历史文化底蕴深厚，具有发展高端制造业和文化产业的优势。以国家中心城市西安为中心的“米”字型交通网加快人口、经济要素等向关中平原城市群集聚，该区域战略性新兴产业发展迅猛，现代服务业快速崛起，产业功能区加快建设，产业结构向中高端迈进，生态保护和高质量发展协同发展表现良好。

5. 晋中城市群

晋中城市群，又被称作山西中部城市群，以山西省太原市为发展中心，以晋中城镇密集区为主体。位于黄河流域中游地区、山西省中部地区和全国“两横三纵”城市化战略格局中京哈京广通道纵轴的中部，是连接东西城市群的“桥梁”，具有良好的区位优势。晋中城市群是我国目前还处于培育阶段的城市群之一，制造业发达，旅游资源丰富，包括世界文化遗产平遥古城、晋商民俗文化旅游区等一批旅游精品，旅游资源优势日益凸显。在中部崛起以及“两横三纵”战略支持下，晋中城

and Gansu, including 11 cities, connecting the upper and middle reaches of the Yellow River, possessing significant economic synergy and strategic position. With a good foundation for development and great potential, the Guanzhong Plain city cluster occupies a unique strategic position in the overall modernization and all-round opening up. It is a key area for traditional energy development, a nationally important base for equipment manufacturing industry, and a high-tech industrial base, where manufacturing industry develops rapidly. It is also the birthplace and prosperous place of the ancestor culture and the Han and Tang cultures, with a profound historical and cultural heritage, and has the advantage of developing high-end manufacturing and cultural industries. Centered around the national central city of Xi'an, the "米" (Mi, a Chinese character)-shaped transportation network is accelerating the aggregation of population and economic factors into the Guanzhong Plain city cluster. This region is experiencing rapid development in strategic emerging industries and a swift rise in modern service industries. Industrial functional zones are being constructed at a faster pace, and the industrial structure is advancing towards mid-to-high-end levels. The region is also demonstrating strong coordination between ecological protection and high-quality collaborative development.

5. Jinzhong City Cluster

Also known as the Central Shanxi city cluster, the Jinzhong city cluster takes Taiyuan City in Shanxi Province as the development center and the densely populated areas of Jinzhong as the main body. Located in the middle reaches of the Yellow River Basin region, central Shanxi Province, and the central axis of the "two horizontal and three vertical" urbanization strategy connecting the Jingha-Jingguang corridor, this area serves as a "bridge" linking eastern and western city clusters, providing excellent locational advantages. The Jinzhong city cluster is currently one of the city clusters in the cultivation stage in China. It has a well-developed manufacturing industry and rich tourism resources, including a collection of premium tourist attractions such as the UNESCO World Heritage Site Pingyao Ancient City and the Jin (abbr. for Shanxi Province) Merchants Folk Culture Tourism Area. The advantage of tourism resources is increasingly prominent. Supported by the rise of central China and the "two horizontal and three vertical" strategy, the Jinzhong city cluster is focusing on transforming its resource-based economy. It aims to build distinctive industrial eco-circles and

市群作为资源经济转型的重点区域，着力打造特色产业生态圈，加快建设城市群产业功能区，其生态保护和经济高质量发展协同水平呈现上升趋势。

6. 中原城市群

中原城市群以河南省郑州市、开封市、洛阳市、平顶山市、新乡市、焦作市、许昌市、漯河市、济源市、鹤壁市、商丘市、周口市以及山西省晋城市、安徽省亳州市为核心发展区，以核心发展区的驱动优势辐射安阳市、濮阳市、三门峡市、南阳市、信阳市、驻马店市、邯郸市、邢台市、长治市、运城市、宿州市、阜阳市、淮北市、蚌埠市、聊城市、菏泽市等中原经济区的其他城市，形成密切的协同推进关系。“十三五”时期，该地区生产总值达 81266 亿，占全国 8.0%。中原城市群借助产业政策和空间布局手段，打破要素流动障碍，提高资源的配置效率，以创新为动力，不断加快新旧动能的转换，发展新兴产业，推动产业结构转型升级，构建现代化产业体系，使城市群逐步转向依靠技术创新的低能耗、低排放、低污染的绿色工业，逐渐成为承东启西、带动中西部地区发展的重要经济地带。作为国家中心城市的郑州，在拉动中原城市群发展方面，也是重要的动力源系统。中原城市群在生态保护和经济高质量发展方面的协同水平稳步提升。

accelerate the construction of industrial functional zones within the city cluster. The region is showing an upward trend in the coordination between ecological protection and high-quality economic development.

6. Central Plains City Cluster

The Central Plains city cluster takes cities of Zhengzhou, Kaifeng, Luoyang, Pingdingshan, Xinxiang, Jiaozuo, Xuchang, Luohe, Jiyuan, Hebi, Shangqiu, Zhoukou in Henan Province, as well as Jincheng City in Shanxi Province, and Bozhou City in Anhui Province as the core development area. It radiates the advantages of the core development area to other cities in the Central Plains Economic Zone such as Anyang, Puyang, Sanmenxia, Nanyang, Xinyang, Zhumadian, Handan, Xingtai, Changzhi, Yuncheng, Suzhou, Fuyang, Huaibei, Bengbu, Liaocheng, Heze, etc., forming a close collaborative promotion relationship. During the "13th Five-Year Plan" period, the region's GDP reached 8,126.6 billion, accounting for 8% of the national total. The Central Plains city cluster, with the help of industrial policies and spatial layout methods, broke the barriers to the flow of factors, improved the efficiency of resource allocation, and took innovation as the driving force. It continuously accelerated the transformation of old and new kinetic energy, developed emerging industries, promoted the transformation and upgrading of the industrial structure, built a modern industrial system, and gradually shifted the city cluster to rely on technological innovation for low-energy, low-emission, and low-pollution green industry. It has gradually become an important economic belt that connects the east and west and drives the development of the central and western regions. As a national central city, Zhengzhou is also an important power source system in driving the development of the Central Plains city cluster. The synergy level of ecological protection and high-quality economic development in the Central Plains city cluster is steadily improving.

7. Shandong Peninsula City Cluster

The Shandong Peninsula city cluster includes all sixteen cities of Shandong Province and is a key area for the development of Shandong Province. As the land-sea junction area where the Yellow River flows into the sea, it has a superior geographical location. It uses its locational advantages to closely engage in trade exchanges with diverse regions and countries, has a high level of opening up to the

7. 山东半岛城市群

山东半岛城市群包含山东全域十六市，是山东省发展的重点区域，作为黄河入海的陆海衔接区域，地理位置优越。利用其区位优势密切与不同地区和国家贸易往来，对外开放水平较高，在拉动整个黄河内陆区域的陆海双向内外联动方面发挥着独有的龙头作用。同时，山东半岛城市群技术、资金密集，具有发展战略性新兴产业和高新技术产业的优势。近年来，山东半岛城市群逐渐突破低端产业主导的瓶颈，加快发展高端信息技术产业，以新旧动能转化作为绿色技术和清洁生产推广应用的驱动力，实现经济发展绿色转型，经济发展水平不断提升。且该城市群基础设施比较完善，交通网络发达，居民幸福指数高，其生态保护和经济高质量发展协同度表现良好。在山东半岛城市群中，济南市作为黄河下游的核心城市，济南新旧动能转换起步区也是继雄安新区之后的全国第二个起步区，担负着打造黄河流域生态保护和高质量发展新示范的重任，贯彻落实黄河流域生态保护和高质量发展战略，加快山东新旧动能转换综合试验区建设，发挥山东半岛城市群龙头作用，复制自由贸易试验区、国家级新区、国家自主创新示范区和全面创新改革试验区经验政策。2022 年 4 月 25 日，国务院正式批复了《济南新旧动能转换起步区建设实施方案》，指明了起步区“五个着力”的建设方向，明确了“一纵一横两核五组团”的空间布局。对标雄安新区，坚持未来眼光、国际标准、黄河特色，济南编制“1+4+16+N”规划体系，搭建起了起步区建设的“四梁八柱”。

沿黄各城市有序加快构建流域合作新空间。目前，沿黄流域各地市

outside world, and plays a unique leading role in driving the bidirectional internal and external linkage of the entire Yellow River Basin region. At the same time, the Shandong Peninsula city cluster is technology and capital intensive, and possesses advantages in developing strategic emerging industries and high-tech industries. In recent years, the Shandong Peninsula city cluster has gradually broken through the bottleneck dominated by low-end industries, accelerated the development of high-end information technology industries, and used the transformation of old and new kinetic energy as the driving force for the promotion and application of green technology and clean production. It has achieved a green transformation of economic development and continuously improved the level of economic development. Moreover, the city cluster has well-developed infrastructure, an advanced transportation network, a high happiness index for residents, and good coordination in ecological protection and high-quality economic development. Among the Shandong Peninsula city cluster, Jinan City is the core city in the lower reaches of the Yellow River, and the Jinan New and Old Kinetic Energy Conversion Pilot Zone is also the second pilot zone in the country after Xiong'an New Area. It bears the important task of creating a new model for ecological protection and high-quality development in the Yellow River Basin region, implementing the strategy of ecological protection and high-quality development in the Yellow River Basin region, accelerating the construction of the comprehensive pilot zone for new and old kinetic energy conversion in Shandong, giving full play to the leading role of the Shandong Peninsula city cluster, and replicating the experience and policies of pilot free trade zones, national-level new areas, national independent innovation demonstration zones, and comprehensive innovation reform pilot zones. On April 25, 2022, the State Council officially approved the "Implementation Plan for the Construction of the Jinan New and Old Kinetic Energy Conversion Pilot Zone", which outlined the "five focuses" of the construction direction of the pilot zone and specified the spatial layout of "one vertical, one horizontal, two cores, and five groups". Modeled after the Xiong'an New Area, Jinan adheres to a future-oriented, international standard, and Yellow River-themed approach, formulating a "1+4+16+N" planning system to build the "Four Beams and Eight Pillars" of the pilot zone construction.

Cities along the Yellow River are orderly accelerating the construction of new spaces for cooperation in the Yellow River Basin. At present, cities along

正在积极探索合作新空间。在晋陕蒙地区，忻州、榆林、鄂尔多斯三市签订了忻榆鄂黄河区域协同发展的框架协议，共同谋划推动雄安－忻州－榆林－鄂尔多斯的高铁项目以及府谷－保德县域合作示范项目等，打造黄河流域晋陕蒙合作金三角。在呼包银榆经济区，十三个成员城市签订了合作框架协议、基础设施建设协议、文化旅游框架协议、大气污染防治合作协议等多个协议。黄河流域各城市群聚合专业智库资源，持续输出研究成果，助力决策。

中心城市引领城市群发展，不仅具有对外影响力、区域资源集聚力和周边带动能力等外向发展特征，也是内涵式发展的城市典范。黄河流域两个中心城市和七个城市群产业的集聚和高效发展，不仅可以为转移劳动力、调整人口空间分布创造条件，也可以辐射和带动黄河流域其他地区，减轻其他地区的发展压力。

三、现存问题

1. 黄河流域沿线城市发展相对滞后

黄河流域城市群存在中心城市与节点城市发展相对滞后的情况。中心城市在城市群中扮演着集聚和辐射的双重角色，对经济产业发展起到重要作用。但与发达地区相比，黄河流域城市群的中心城市规模和龙头带动作用相对较有限。比如说，关中平原城市群仅包含一个区域中心城

the Yellow River Basin region are actively exploring new spaces for cooperation. In the Shanxi, Shaanxi, and Inner Mongolia regions, Xinzhou, Yulin, and Ordos have signed a framework agreement for the collaborative development of the Yellow River Basin region, jointly planning to promote high-speed rail projects such as Xiong'an-Xinzhou-Yulin-Ordos, as well as county-level cooperation demonstration projects such as Fugu-Baode, etc., to create a golden triangle of cooperation among Shanxi, Shaanxi, and Inner Mongolia in the Yellow River Basin region. In the Hohhot-Baotou-Yinchuan-Yulin economic zone, thirteen member cities have signed multiple agreements, including a cooperation framework agreement, infrastructure construction agreement, cultural tourism framework agreement, and air pollution prevention and control agreement. The city clusters in the Yellow River Basin region have pooled professional think tank resources to continuously output research findings, assisting in decision-making.

Central cities lead the development of city clusters, not only possessing external development characteristics such as external influence, regional resource aggregation, and peripheral driving capabilities, but also serving as models for intensive urban development. The agglomeration and efficient development of the two central cities and seven city clusters in the Yellow River Basin region can not only create conditions for transferring labor and adjusting the spatial distribution of the population but also radiate and drive other areas in the Yellow River Basin region, alleviating the development pressure on other regions.

III. Existing Problems

1.Comparative Lag in the Development of Cities Along the Yellow River Basin Region

There is a relative lag in the development of central and nodal cities in the city clusters of the Yellow River Basin region. Central cities play a dual role in aggregation and radiation within the city clusters, which is crucial for economic and industrial development. However, compared to developed areas, the scale and leading role of central cities in the city clusters of the Yellow River Basin region are relatively limited. For example, the Guanzhong Plain city cluster only includes one regional central city—Xi'an, and its radiation range is limited. Unlike

市——西安，且其辐射范围有限，不像上海等国际都市，可以拉动周边一大片城市的发展。现代城市扩张呈现的变化是一个复杂而多样化的现象，与过去单一中心城市对外密度递减的蔓延模式相比，现在更多地出现了区域内多个节点城市在城市功能分区上形成的多中心集聚模式。这种多中心集聚模式在推动产业结构演进方面发挥着重要作用。通过在不同城市节点培育不同的产业重点，可以实现产业结构的优化和升级。不同城市节点之间的专业化分工，有助于提高整个区域的产业效率和创新能力。然而，在黄河流域这片广阔的土地上，虽然存在着一些城市群，但大部分城市群都没有明显的节点城市，即在城市群内具有引领和集聚作用的核心城市。这种缺乏节点城市的情况造成了城市群之间联系的薄弱，限制了区域内产业、人才和资源的流动与融合。

2. 区域内交通网络不完善

交通建设相对滞后，可能导致区域内交通网络的不完善和发展的阻碍。黄河流域地理空间较远，包含的地域广阔，导致不同地区之间的交通和物流成本相对较高。这使得资源的配置和经济活动的开展相对受限，影响了区域内经济活动的密度和效率。较远的地理距离也可能导致市场相对疏弱，难以形成良好的市场规模，制约了区域内产业的集聚和发展。因此，在黄河流域城市群的发展过程中，高效的城际交通联系起着至关重要的作用。畅通的交通网络可以促进人员、物资和信息的快速流动，有利于加强城市之间的合作与互动，提升经济发展的整体效率。同时，较低的交通运输成本可以降低物流和交通费用，激发投资和创业

international cities such as Shanghai, it can drive the development of a large surrounding area. The expansion of modern cities presents a complex and diverse phenomenon. Compared with the past pattern of single central city expansion with decreasing density outward, there are now more polycentric agglomeration models formed by multiple nodal cities within the region in terms of urban functional zoning. This polycentric agglomeration model plays an important role in promoting the evolution of the industrial structure. By cultivating different industrial focuses in different urban nodes, the optimization and upgrading of the industrial structure can be achieved. The specialized division of labor between different urban nodes helps to improve the industrial efficiency and innovation capacity of the entire region. However, in the vast land of the Yellow River Basin region, although there are some urban clusters, most of them do not have obvious nodal cities, that is, core cities with leading and agglomerating effects within the urban clusters. The lack of nodal cities has led to weak connections between city clusters, restricting the flow and integration of industries, talents, and resources within the region.

2.Underdeveloped Transportation Network in the Region

The underdeveloped transportation network in the region may lead to the imperfection and obstruction of the perfection of the regional transportation network. The Yellow River Basin region has a long geographical space and covers a vast area, resulting in relatively high transportation and logistics costs between different regions. This limits the allocation of resources and the conduct of economic activities, affecting the density and efficiency of economic activities within the region. The longer geographical distance may also lead to relatively weak market, making it difficult to form a good market size, which restricts the agglomeration and development of industries within the region. Therefore, in the development process of the city clusters in the Yellow River Basin region, efficient intercity transportation links play a crucial role.A smooth transportation network can promote the rapid flow of personnel, materials, and information, which is conducive to strengthening cooperation and interaction between cities, and improving the overall efficiency of economic development. At the same time, lower transportation costs can reduce logistics and transportation expenses, stimulate investment and entrepreneurship enthusiasm, and promote

的积极性，促进资源的合理配置和市场的扩大。然而，黄河流域的高铁建设目前还存在一些挑战。首先，由于地域广阔，高铁建设需要巨大的投资和资源，但受限于经济发展水平和资金供给，该地区高铁线路的铺设仍然相对滞后。其次，缺乏全面的区域合作也是一个制约因素，黄河流域涉及多个省份和地区，要形成覆盖面广的高铁交通网需要各方的协调和合作。

3. 产业分工与空间双向抑制现象

黄河流域城市群的建设面临着产业分工与空间的双向抑制现象。首先，由于历史发展和资源禀赋的差异，不同城市在产业结构上存在明显差异。一些城市可能在特定产业领域有明显的优势，形成了一定程度的产业集聚效应，但同时也使得其他城市在该领域难以进入或竞争力较弱。产业分工的双向抑制也可能造成某些产业过度集中在个别城市，导致资源过度集中、环境压力增大等问题。这种过度集中可能会导致中心城市过度繁荣，而周边城市缺乏发展动力，产业空心化现象加剧。其次，空间的双向抑制也是一个重要因素。黄河流域城市群的城市分布相对分散，地域广阔，城市之间的距离较远。这种空间分散可能会导致交通成本和物流成本的增加，阻碍资源和产业的有效流动，限制了城市间合作与协同发展。同时，城市间的空间距离也可能影响人才流动和信息传播，造成资源和技术的局部化积累，阻碍了区域创新和竞争力的提升。这种现象需要引起重视，通过促进区域间合作与交流，加强交通基础设施建设，打破市场分割，才能推动黄河流域城市群的产业和城市空

the rational allocation of resources and market expansion. However, there are still some challenges in the construction of high-speed railways in the Yellow River Basin region at present. Firstly, due to the vast territory, the construction of high-speed railways requires huge investment and resources, but it is still relatively lagging in the layout of high-speed railway lines in the area due to the limitations of economic development level and capital supply. Secondly, the lack of comprehensive regional cooperation is also a constraining factor. The Yellow River Basin region involves multiple provinces and regions, and the formation of a widely covered high-speed railway transportation network requires coordination and cooperation from all parties.

3. The Mutual Inhibition Between Industrial Division and Spatial Distribution

The construction of city clusters in the Yellow River Basin region is facing the mutual inhibition between industrial division and spatial distribution. Firstly, due to the differences in historical development and resource endowment, there are obvious differences in the industrial structure of different cities. Some cities may have a clear advantage in a specific industrial field, forming a certain degree of industrial agglomeration effect, but at the same time, it also makes it difficult for other cities to enter or have weaker competitiveness in this field. The dual inhibition of industrial division may also cause some industries to be overly concentrated in individual cities, leading to problems such as excessive concentration of resources and increased environmental pressure. This over-concentration may lead to excessive prosperity of central cities, while surrounding cities lack development momentum, and the phenomenon of industrial hollowing out is exacerbated. Secondly, the dual inhibition of spatial development is also an important factor. The cities in the city clusters of the Yellow River Basin region are relatively dispersed, with vast areas and relatively long distances between cities. This spatial dispersion may lead to increased transportation and logistics costs, hindering the effective flow of resources and industries, and limiting cooperation and collaborative development between cities. At the same time, the spatial distance between cities may also affect the flow of talent and the dissemination of information, leading to localized accumulation of resources and technology, and hindering regional innovation and competitiveness. This phenomenon needs to be

间的协调发展。

4. 区域发展不协调

黄河流域城市群之间存在明显的发展差异，这种差异导致了区域发展的不协调，表现在多个方面。由于各城市群所处区域的区位条件、自然环境和发育基础等因素不同，不同城市之间的产业结构和经济特色存在较大差异。因地理位置、资源禀赋和历史因素的影响，黄河流域城市群内的城市可能专注于不同的产业领域。这使得一些城市在特定产业方面有明显的优势，而其他城市则可能缺乏相关产业支撑，导致区域产业布局不均衡。尚未形成有效的协调机制，使得黄河流域城市群要实现协调发展存在一定难度。为了解决这一问题，需要加强不同区域之间的合作与交流，推动资源的优化配置和产业的互补发展，以促进黄河流域城市群的协调与共同繁荣。

四、解决路径

（1）针对沿线城市发展相对滞后问题。在中心城市发展、都市圈形成、产业协同发展和城市群间合作等方面采取综合性的政策措施，以实现区域经济的协调发展和全面繁荣。通过推进资本、劳动力等生产要素的持续聚集，提升生产和服务业的发展水平，实现中心城市的劳动生产率提升并充分发挥其辐射效应，将为周边城市的产业转型和升级带来积极推动作用，促进整个区域经济的协调发展。这样的良性循环将推动区域内城市的共同繁荣与可持续发展。都市圈作为城市群内部的一部分，主要形成以“1 小时经济圈”为定位的发展模式，旨在加强区域内城市

taken seriously. Only by promoting cooperation and exchange between regions, strengthening the construction of transportation infrastructure, and breaking market segmentation, can the coordinated development of industries and urban space in the city clusters of the Yellow River Basin region be promoted.

4.Uncoordinated Regional Development

There are significant development differences between the city clusters in the Yellow River Basin region, which have led to uncoordinated regional development phenomena, manifested in various aspects. Due to different locational conditions, natural environments, and developmental foundations of the areas where each city cluster is located, there are considerable differences in the industrial structure and economic characteristics between different cities. Influenced by geographical location, resource endowment, and historical factors, cities within the Yellow River Basin region city clusters may focus on different industrial sectors. This allows some cities to have obvious advantages in specific industries, while other cities may lack relevant industrial support, leading to an unbalanced regional industrial layout. An effective coordination mechanism has not yet been formed, making it difficult for the city clusters in the Yellow River Basin region to achieve coordinated development. To address this issue, it is necessary to strengthen cooperation and exchange between different regions, promote the optimal allocation of resources and the complementary development of industries, to foster the coordination and joint prosperity of the city clusters in the Yellow River Basin region.

IV. Feasible Solutions

(1) To address the comparative lag in the development of cities along the Yellow River Basin region. Comprehensive policy measures should be adopted in the development of central cities, the formation of metropolitan areas, industrial collaborative development, and cooperation between city clusters to achieve coordinated regional economic development and overall prosperity. By promoting the continuous aggregation of capital, labor, and other production factors, enhancing the development level of production and service industries, and realizing the increase in labor productivity in central cities while fully leveraging their radiative effects, this will positively drive the transformation and upgrading

之间的联系与合作，推动资源优化配置和产业协同发展，从而实现整个黄河流域城市群的经济繁荣与可持续发展。因此，逐步形成“中心城市－都市圈－城市群”的空间结构，构建高标准的黄河流域城市群是十分重要的。在这个空间结构下，城市群内部将形成良好的经济合作与发展模式，有助于实现整体经济的协调和繁荣。

（2）针对区域内交通网络不完善问题。推进城际高效互通的交通网络建设。为此，需要加快黄河流域城市间高速公路、高速铁路等交通基础设施的建设，以提高城市群交通网络的密度和连接效率，从而促进经济一体化、资源优化配置和区域协调发展。同时，加大对黄河流域经济基础相对较弱的城市的基础设施扶持力度，促进周边城市的整体发展，是实现区域经济协调发展的重要措施。通过这些措施，可以促进城市群之间的联系和合作，推动区域经济的协调发展。高效的城际交通联系和畅通的交通网络可以促进人员、物资和信息的快速流动，有利于加强城市之间的合作与互动，提升经济发展的整体效率。同时，较低的交通运输成本可以降低物流和交通费用，激发投资和创业的积极性，促进资源的合理配置和市场的扩大。然而，黄河流域的高铁建设目前还存在一些挑战。首先，由于地域广阔，高铁建设需要巨大的投资和资源，但受限

of industries in surrounding cities and promote the coordinated development of the entire regional economy. Such a virtuous cycle will drive the shared prosperity and sustainable development of cities within the region. As part of the city cluster, the metropolitan area mainly adopts a development model positioned around the "one-hour economic circle". The goal is to strengthen the connection and cooperation between cities in the region, promote optimized resource allocation, and foster synergistic development of industries. This, in turn, will lead to economic prosperity and sustainable development for the entire Yellow River Basin region city clusters. Therefore, it is very crucial to gradually form a spatial structure of "central city-metropolitan area-city cluster" and construct a high-standard city cluster in the Yellow River Basin region. Within this spatial structure, the city cluster will foster a beneficial economic cooperation and development model internally, contributing to the overall economic coordination and prosperity.

(2) To address the issue of imperfect regional transportation network. Promote the construction of an efficient intercity transportation network. To this end, it is necessary to accelerate the construction of transportation infrastructure such as expressways and high-speed railways between cities in the Yellow River Basin region, in order to improve the density and connectivity of the city cluster's transportation network, thereby promoting economic integration, optimal allocation of resources, and coordinated regional development. At the same time, increasing support for infrastructure in cities with relatively weak economic foundations in the Yellow River Basin region and promoting the overall development of surrounding cities are important measures to achieve coordinated regional economic development. Through these measures, connections and cooperation between city clusters can be promoted, driving coordinated regional economic development. Efficient intercity transportation links and smooth traffic networks can promote the rapid flow of people, materials, and information, which is conducive to strengthening cooperation and interaction between cities, and improving the overall efficiency of economic development. At the same time, lower transportation costs can reduce logistics and transportation expenses, stimulate investment and entrepreneurial enthusiasm, and promote the rational allocation of resources and market expansion. However, there are still some

于经济发展水平和资金供给，该地区高铁线路的铺设仍然相对滞后。其次，缺乏全面的区域合作也是一个制约因素，黄河流域涉及多个省份和地区，要形成覆盖面广的高铁交通网需要各方的协调和合作。

（3）针对产业分工与空间双向抑制现象，通过促进区域间合作与交流，加强交通基础设施建设，打破市场分割，推动黄河流域城市群的产业和城市空间的协调发展。同时通过调整黄河流域的产业政策取向，可以为建设高标准城市群提供制度保障路径，推动区域经济的高质量发展和城市群的可持续繁荣。通过推动城市群建设政策设计从选择性产业政策转向集聚政策，可以为黄河流域城市群的发展提供更有力的支持和保障。这意味着要在政策层面上鼓励城市群内部产业的深度分工与协作，制定差异化的产业支持政策，实现错位发展，避免产业趋同，从而推动城市群内各城市的经济协同发展和差异化优势的形成。同时，为了促进区域产业的协调发展，需要突破行政区划的束缚，并对考核和管理体制进行必要的改革。构建城市群产业协作的长效机制是至关重要的一步。这一长效机制可以促进各城市之间产业资源的优势互补，实现产业链的高效衔接和协同创新。通过跨城市合作，可以提高区域产业的整体竞争力，形成合力抢占市场份额，提高产品和服务的质量水平，满足消费者多样化的需求。这样的制度保障路径可以为城市群的建设提供有效的支持，推动黄河流域城市群向高标准发展迈进。

（4）针对区域发展不协调现象，应该在规划和发展城市群时，充分

challenges in the construction of high-speed railways in the Yellow River Basin region. Firstly, due to the vast territory, the construction of high-speed railways requires huge investment and resources, but it is still relatively lagging in the layout of high-speed railway lines in the area due to the limitations of economic development level and capital supply. Secondly, the lack of comprehensive regional cooperation is also a constraining factor. The Yellow River Basin involves multiple provinces and regions, and the formation of a widely covered high-speed railway network requires coordination and cooperation from all parties.

(3) To address the mutual inhibition between industrial division and spatial distribution. Promoting regional cooperation and communication, strengthening the construction of transportation infrastructure, breaking down market barriers will drive the coordinated development of industries and city spaces in the Yellow River Basin region city clusters. Simultaneously, by adjusting the industrial policy orientation in the Yellow River Basin region, a path of institutional guarantee can be provided for building high-standard city clusters, promoting high-quality development of the regional economy and sustainable prosperity of the city cluster. Shifting the focus of city cluster construction policies from selective industrial policies to cluster policies can provide stronger support and guarantees for the development of the Yellow River Basin region city clusters. This means encouraging deep specialization and collaboration among industries within the city cluster at the policy level, formulating differentiated industrial support policies, achieving differentiated development, avoiding industrial convergence, and thereby promoting the economic synergistic development of cities within the city cluster and the formation of differentiated advantages. Moreover, to promote the coordinated development of regional industries, it is necessary to break through administrative boundaries and carry out necessary reforms in assessment and management systems. Establishing a long-term mechanism for industrial cooperation within city clusters is a crucial step. This mechanism can promote complementary advantages in industrial resources among cities, achieve efficient linkage of industrial chains, and foster collaborative innovation. Through intercity cooperation, overall competitiveness of regional industries can be enhanced, joint efforts can be made to capture market share, product and service quality can be improved, and diverse consumer demands can be met. Such a pathway for ensuring institutional safeguards can provide effective support for urban

考虑黄河流域上、中、下游的生态环境差异，因为不同流域段的特点各异，对于生态环境的保护和发展要求也会有所不同。对于上游地区，通常具有较为原始和自然的生态环境，因此，在城市群的规划中，应该优先考虑生态保护，确保上游地区的生态系统得到有效的保护和恢复，同时注重发展具有当地特色的生态旅游和生态农业等可持续发展产业。中游地区，由于位于黄河流域的中部，其生态环境面临着更多的挑战。在城市群规划中，需要综合考虑生态保护和经济发展的平衡。在保护生态环境的同时，积极推进绿色产业和低碳发展，以实现生态和经济的双赢。至于下游地区，由于其靠近黄河入海口，其生态环境特点和压力与上中游地区有所不同。在城市群规划中，需要重视防洪防涝和海洋生态保护，并在城市建设和产业发展中采取更多的生态友好措施。

综上所述，在黄河流域城市和城市群高质量发展的过程中，应该以生态保护为优先，需要在构建城市群绿色发展空间格局的过程中，强化功能分区指导，同时加强不同区域之间的合作与交流，推动资源的优化配置和产业的互补发展，以促进黄河流域城市群的协调与共同繁荣。

agglomeration construction and propel the Yellow River Basin region city cluster towards high-standard development.

(4) To address the phenomenon of uncoordinated regional development. When planning and developing city clusters, it is necessary to fully consider the ecological environment differences of the upper, middle, and lower reaches of the Yellow River Basin region, as the characteristics of different basin sections vary, and the requirements for ecological environment protection and development will also differ. For the upper reaches, which usually have a more pristine and natural ecological environment, in the planning of city clusters, priority should be given to ecological protection to ensure that the ecosystem of the upper reaches is effectively protected and restored, while also focusing on the development of sustainable industries with local characteristics, such as ecological tourism and ecological agriculture. In the middle reaches, due to its location in the middle of the Yellow River Basin region, the ecological environment faces more challenges. In the planning of city clusters, it is necessary to consider a balance between ecological protection and economic development. While protecting the ecological environment, actively promote green industries and low-carbon development to achieve a win-win situation for ecology and economy. As for the lower reaches, due to its proximity to the estuary of the Yellow River, its ecological environment characteristics and pressures are different from those of the upper and middle reaches. In the planning of city clusters, it is necessary to pay attention to flood control and marine ecological protection, and adopt more eco-friendly measures in urban construction and industrial development.

In summary, in the process of high-quality development of cities and city clusters in the Yellow River Basin region, ecological protection should be given priority. It is necessary to strengthen functional zoning guidance in the process of building a green development spatial pattern for city clusters, while enhancing cooperation and exchange between different regions, promoting the optimal allocation of resources and the complementary development of industries, to promote the coordination and common prosperity of city clusters in the Yellow River Basin region.

第五章

科技创新驱动高质量发展

Chapter 5

Sci-Tech Innovation Driving High-quality Development

一、创新资源集聚

科技创新作为全面塑造新发展优势的重要支点，是实现黄河流域高质量发展的核心驱动力。随着黄河流域生态保护和高质量发展升级为重大国家战略，黄河流域科技创新水平逐年提升，创新资源与要素纷纷涌入，创新示范平台不断完善，数字技术应用逐渐广泛，创新驱动高质量发展取得卓越成就。近年来，黄河流域各省区逐步强化科技创新对黄河流域经济社会高质量发展的支撑引领作用，并取得了长足进步。在2022年中国区域创新能力评价中，黄河流域的山东、陕西两省跻身前十位，四川、河南两省分别为第12、13位，流域整体创新步伐不断加快。

黄河流域创新驱动效果显著，2022年黄河流域人均GDP为71551.22元，城乡居民人均可支配收入之比为2.48，环境空气质量优良天数比例为81.17%，单位生产总值能耗不断降低；黄河流域创新环境不断完善，创新人才培养意识逐步加强，采取多项科技管理新举措，整体科技布局渐趋优化，2022年教育经费占GDP比重为3.30%，教育支出占财政预算支出比重约为17.05%；黄河流域科技创新成绩斐然，截至2022年，黄河流域共有高新技术企业6万余家，九省区2022年专利授权量为63.78万件，技术市场成交额7858.82亿元。

I. Agglomeration of Innovation Resources

Technological innovation, as an important fulcrum for comprehensively shaping new development advantages, is the core driving force for achieving high-quality development in the Yellow River Basin region. As ecological protection and high-quality development in the Yellow River Basin region have been upgraded to a major national strategy, the level of technological innovation in the Yellow River Basin region has been increasing year by year. Innovation resources and elements have been pouring in, innovative demonstration platforms have been continuously improved, the application of digital technology has gradually become more extensive, and innovation has made outstanding achievements in driving high-quality development. In recent years, the provinces and regions of the Yellow River Basin region have gradually strengthened the supporting and leading role of technological innovation in the high-quality economic and social development of the Yellow River Basin region, and have made significant progress. In the 2022 China Regional Innovation Capacity Evaluation, Shandong and Shaanxi provinces in the Yellow River Basin region ranked in the top ten, while Sichuan and Henan provinces ranked 12th and 13th respectively, with the overall pace of innovation in the basin continuously accelerating.

The innovation-driven effect in the Yellow River Basin region is remarkable. In 2022, the per capita GDP of the Yellow River Basin region was 71,551.22 yuan, the ratio of disposable income per capita between urban and rural residents was 2.48, the proportion of good air quality days was 81.17%, and the energy consumption per unit of GDP continued to decrease. The innovation environment in the Yellow River Basin region is continuously improving, the awareness of innovative talent cultivation is gradually strengthening, and a number of new scientific and technological management measures have been taken, making the overall scientific and technological layout increasingly optimized. In 2022, the proportion of educational expenditure in GDP was 3.30%, and the proportion of educational expenditure in fiscal budgetary expenditure was about 17.05%. The Yellow River Basin region has achieved remarkable results in scientific and technological innovation. By the end of 2022, there were more than 60,000 high-tech enterprises in the Yellow River Basin region, with 637,800 patent

1. 高水平人才与高等教育

人才是科技创新的第一资源，其创新意识与能力能够在根本上决定科技创新的发展速度和水平。2022 年，黄河流域高等教育在校生人数为 1165.25 万人，R&D 人员全时当量共有 73.46 万人，其中山东省的研究与开发人员数量最多，陕西省硕士、博士毕业生比例最高。此外，黄河流域还紧紧围绕水资源集约节约利用、生态环境治理、自然灾害防御等方面培育了一批知识型、技能型、创新型的黄河工匠，为深入推进黄河流域生态保护和高质量发展提供高素质人才支撑。

高校作为人才培养的重镇和科学研究的主流阵地，对地区的人才竞争力的培养至关重要。黄河流域共有普通高等院校 757 所，“双一流”高校 26 所，每十万人高等教育平均在校生人数达到 2392 人。过去的几

郑州大学（“双一流”建设高校）
Zhengzhou University (Included in “Double First-Class Project”)

authorizations in 2022 across the nine provinces and regions, and the technical market transaction volume reached 785.882 billion yuan.

1.High-Level Talent and Higher Education

Talent is the first resource of scientific and technological innovation, and their awareness and ability of innovation can fundamentally determine the speed and level of scientific and technological innovation development. In 2022, the number of students in higher education in the Yellow River Basin region was 11.6525 million, and the full-time equivalent of R&D personnel was 734,600, of which Shandong Province had the largest number of research and development personnel, and Shaanxi Province had the highest proportion of master's and doctoral graduates. In addition, the Yellow River Basin region has also focused on cultivating a group of knowledgeable, skilled, and innovative Yellow River craftsmen in areas such as intensive and economical use of water resources, ecological environment management, and natural disaster prevention, providing high-quality talent support for the in-depth promotion of ecological protection and high-quality development in the Yellow River Basin region.

Universities, as key bases for talent cultivation and main positions for scientific research, are crucial for cultivating the competitiveness of regional talent. There are a total of 757 general colleges and universities in the Yellow River Basin region, including 26 "Double First-Class" universities, with an average of 2,392 students in higher education per 100,000 people. In the past few years, universities in the Yellow River Basin region have accelerated the development of first-class universities and disciplines, and have closely cooperated with government departments and research institutions. Focusing on the theme of ecological protection and high-quality development in the Yellow River Basin region, they have carried out work in scientific research platform construction, project application, and talent training, actively connecting with major Yellow River management projects, providing superior solutions for the high-quality economic and social development of the Yellow River Basin region.

2. Innovation Platforms

As a gathering place for innovative elements, technological innovation platforms are important carriers for promoting the transfer and transformation of scientific and technological achievements, and for cultivating and developing

年间，黄河流域高校纷纷加快一流大学和一流学科的培育建设步伐，并与政府部门、研究机构密切合作，紧紧围绕黄河流域生态保护和高质量发展这一主题，在科研平台建设、项目申报、人才培养等方面开展工作，主动对接重大治黄项目，为黄河流域经济社会高质量发展提供了优质的解决方案。

2. 创新平台

科技创新平台作为创新要素的汇聚地，是促进科技成果转移转化和培育发展高新技术产业的重要载体。黄河流域各省区为解决在发展过程中存在的“卡脖子”问题，统筹科技研发平台建设，紧紧围绕水资源高效利用、产业转型、低碳发展等方面着力突破共性核心技术。2021 年济南提出将联合沿黄九省区打造黄河科技创新联盟，建设黄河科创走廊，同年 12 月，沿黄省区发出共同倡议，表示将借助科创联盟，共建科创平台、协同攻关、共同促进科技成果转化。

在科技成果产业化平台方面，黄河流域也表现出不凡的实力。据统计，2022 年黄河流域拥有省级开发区共计 744 个，占全国省级开发区数量的 26.80%，国家经济技术开发区 52 家，占全国国家经济技术开发区数量的 22.61%，国家高新技术开发区 45 个，占全国国家高新技术开发区数量的 26.63%，综合保税区 39 个，占全国综合保税区数量的 23.21%。黄河流域整体产业化平台建设卓有成效，已然成为我国科技成果转化领域的重要区域，为我国科技创新、产业结构优化进程做出了巨大贡献。除了流域整体平台建设，各省区的创新平台建设工作也在持续深入推进。河南省规划筹建国家生物育种产业创新中心，并在不到一年的时间内密集揭牌了由郑州大学、河南大学、河南农业大学等高校牵头打造的嵩山实验室，由黄河水利委员会、郑州大学牵头成立的黄河实验室，以及省级中试基地、省级产业研究院等一流创新平台，充分满足了河南省对高端创新要素的迫切需求。山西省也毫不逊色，近年来接连获批设立了怀柔国家实验室山西基地，国家超算（太原）中心、国家第三

high-tech industries. To address the "bottleneck" issues in the development process, provinces and regions in the Yellow River Basin region have coordinated the construction of scientific and technological R&D platforms, focusing on breaking through common core technologies in aspects such as efficient use of water resources, industrial transformation, and low-carbon development. In 2021, Jinan proposed to establish the Yellow River Science and Technology Innovation Alliance jointly with nine provinces and regions along the Yellow River, and to build the Yellow River Science and Innovation Corridor. In December of the same year, provinces and regions along the Yellow River jointly issued a proposal, stating that they would leverage the Science and Technology Innovation Alliance to jointly build a science and technology innovation platform, collaborate on tackling key issues, and promote the transformation of scientific and technological achievements.

In terms of platforms for the industrialization of scientific and technological achievements, the Yellow River Basin region also shows remarkable strength. According to statistics, in 2022, the Yellow River Basin region had a total of 744 provincial-level development zones, accounting for 26.80% of the national total, 52 national economic and technological development zones, accounting for 22.61% of the national total, 45 national high-tech development zones, accounting for 26.63% of the national total, and 39 integrated free trade zones, accounting for 23.21% of the national total. The overall construction of industrialization platforms in the Yellow River Basin region has been highly effective and it has become an important region in China's field of scientific and technological achievement transformation, making a significant contribution to China's technological innovation and industrial structure optimization. In addition to the construction of an overall platform in the Yellow River Basin, the construction of innovation platforms in each province and region is also continuing to be advanced deeply. Henan Province planned and initiated the establishment of the National Innovation Center for Biological Breeding Industry. In less than a year, it unveiled several high-level innovation platforms, including the Song Mountain Laboratory led by Zhengzhou University, Henan University, and Henan Agricultural University, as well as the Yellow River Laboratory led by the Yellow River Conservancy Commission and Zhengzhou University. These

代半导体技术创新中心（山西）获批并成功运行，立项筹建多个省级实验室。

郑州大学国家大学科技园
The National University Science and Technology Park of Zhengzhou University

3. 研发资金投入

研发资金是科技创新活动的血液和物质基础，资金配置效率深刻地影响着科技对高质量发展的促进作用。2022 年黄河流域科技财政支出为 1571.55 亿元，占财政预算支出总额的 2.64%，在 2021 年基础上提升了 309.06 亿元，增速约为 24.48%。R&D 经费共计 5245.39 亿元，研发强度为 1.71%，规模以上工业企业新产品开发经费支出为 4216.35 亿元，较 2021 年增长 13.05%，黄河流域政府资金投入金额虽然在逐年递增，但是其速度小于全社会的研究经费投入，这说明财政资金的杠杆效应逐渐凸显，更多的社会资本进入科技创新活动领域之中来。此外，黄河流

platforms, along with provincial-level pilot bases and industrial research institutes, fully meet the urgent demand for high-end innovation elements in Henan Province. Shanxi Province is also making remarkable progress. In recent years, it has successively established the Huairou National Laboratory Shanxi Base, the National Supercomputing Center (Taiyuan), and the National Third-Generation Semiconductor Technology Innovation Center (Shanxi), all of which have been approved and are running successfully. Additionally, several provincial-level laboratories are being planned and established.

3. Research and Development (R&D) Funding Investment

R&D funding is the lifeblood and material basis of scientific and technological innovation activities, and the efficiency of capital allocation profoundly affects the role of science and technology in promoting high-quality development. In 2022, the scientific and technological financial expenditure of the Yellow River Basin region was 157.155 billion yuan, accounting for 2.64% of the total financial budgetary expenditure, an increase of 30.906 billion yuan from 2021, with a growth rate of about 24.48%. The R&D funding totaled 524.539 billion yuan, with a research and development intensity of 1.71%. The expenditure on new product development by large-scale industrial enterprises above the designated size was 421.635 billion yuan, an increase of 13.05% compared to 2021. Although the government funding in the Yellow River Basin region is increasing year by year, the rate of increase is less than that of the total R&D investment in society, indicating that the leverage effect of fiscal funds is gradually highlighting, and more social capital is entering the field of scientific and technological innovation activities. Furthermore, the Yellow River Basin has actively developed green finance, improved tax policies, and increased government procurement efforts, laying a solid economic foundation for enhancing the overall technological innovation level in the Yellow River Basin.

While increasing investment in scientific and technological innovation, the governments of the provinces and regions in the Yellow River Basin region have adopted a variety of fiscal incentive measures to encourage technological innovation and have achieved remarkable results. Taking the Ningxia Hui Autonomous Region as an example, since the implementation of the "post-subsidy policy for scientific and technological innovation", nearly 3,600 enterprises have

域还积极发展绿色金融，完善税收政策、加大政府采购力度，为提升黄河流域整体技术创新水平打下了坚实的经济基础。

在加大科技创新资金投入的同时，黄河流域各省区政府采取多样化的财政激励措施鼓励科技创新，并取得了傲人的成绩。以宁夏回族自治区为例，“科技创新后补助”政策自施行以来，为将近3600余家企业提供补助，补助金额逾22亿元，尤其是2021年，补助企业数量再创新高，补助金额也突破了6亿元，其中半数以上都是科技型企业，这在很大程度上缓解了企业创新资金纾困的难题，对于提高企业的创新积极性具有重要影响。

二、创新示范引领

实施创新驱动发展战略是黄河流域生态保护和高质量发展的核心内容。黄河流域拥有国家自主创新示范区4家，农业高新技术示范区2家，作为高新技术发展及相应体制机制改革的先行先试区域，示范区建设对推动黄河流域创新驱动发展及完善相关政策体系具有重要的引领、带动作用。

1. 国家自主创新示范区

（1）兰白国家自主创新示范区

兰白国家自主创新示范区（以下简称“兰白自创区”）于2018年2月经国务院批复设立，由兰州高新技术开发区、白银高新技术开发区组成，是我国西部首个国家自主创新示范区，也是黄河流域上游地区唯一的国家自创区。兰白自创区的设立对于推动甘肃省与黄河流域创新驱动高质量发展具有重要意义，是推进“一带一路”建设、打造向西开放的重要支点，也是欠发达地区依靠创新实现跨越发展的新模式探索。

近年来，甘肃省政府高度重视兰白自创区的发展，制定了《关于支持兰州白银国家自主创新示范区建设的若干意见》《关于进一步支持兰

been subsidized, with a total subsidy amount of more than 2.2 billion yuan. Especially in 2021, the number of subsidized enterprises reached a new high, and the total subsidy amount exceeded 600 million yuan, more than half of which were technology enterprises. This has greatly alleviated the problem of financial difficulties for enterprise innovation and has had an important impact on improving the enthusiasm for enterprise innovation.

II. Leading by Innovation Demonstration

Implementing the strategy of innovation-driven development is a core element of ecological protection and high-quality development in the Yellow River Basin region. The Yellow River Basin region has 4 national independent innovation demonstration zones and 2 high-tech agricultural demonstration zones. As pilot areas for the development of high-tech and corresponding institutional and mechanism reforms, the construction of demonstration zones plays an important leading and driving role in promoting innovation-driven development and improving the relevant policy system in the Yellow River Basin region.

1.National Independent Innovation Demonstration Zones

(1) Lanzhou-Baiyin National Independent Innovation Demonstration Zone

The Lanzhou-Baiyin National Independent Innovation Demonstration Zone (hereinafter referred to as "Lan-Bai Self-innovation Zone") was established in February 2018 with the approval of the State Council, composed of Lanzhou High-tech Industrial Development Zone and Baiyin High-tech Industrial Development Zone. It is the first national independent innovation demonstration zone in the western region of China and the only national self-innovation zone in the upper reaches of the Yellow River Basin region. The establishment of the Lan-Bai Self-innovation Zone is of great significance for promoting the innovation-driven high-quality development of Gansu Province and the Yellow River Basin region. It is an important fulcrum for advancing the "Belt and Road" initiative and creating an opening to the west, as well as a new model exploration for less developed areas to achieve leapfrog development through innovation.

In recent years, the Gansu Provincial Government has attached great

州新区深化改革创新推动高质量发展的意见》等一系列政策文件，分别构建了“1+4+7”和“3+2+10”创新驱动政策体系，设立兰白基金，扩大对社会资本的吸引力度，采取多样化的财政政策支持兰白自创区的发展。兰白两区紧跟国家科技发展前沿，打造“甘肃省能源装备”“甘肃省绿色智慧公路交通”等企业创新联合体；围绕装备制造、信息技术、生物医药等领域，认定22个省级工程研究中心，融合打造创新生态。兰洽会、科博会吸引中国生物、广药集团、华为技术等知名500强企业落户区内，提升甘肃高端产业水平。2022年，兰白两区地区生产总值达1233亿元，占全省总数的11%以上，较上年增长7%；高新技术企业759家，占全省总数的45%，集聚了全省近29%的战略性新型骨干企业和41%的上市企业。此外，兰白自创区充分发挥黄河流域特色，积极对接上海张江国家自主创新示范区，双方成立工作小组，共同搭建张江兰白科技创新改革试验区技术转移中心等多个平台，联合举办“兰州科技博览会”等活动，共同开展科研攻关及成果转化。兰白两区还积极引入上海、河南、福建等地的优质创新资源落户甘肃，积极推进国内首台套标准熔盐泵测试装置、可反复使用防控口罩、低温纤膏应用等一批科技成果在兰白新区快速应用。

（2）西安国家自主创新示范区

西安国家自主创新示范区（以下简称“西安自创区”）成立于2015年6月，地处黄河中游的陕西省，是黄河流域第一家国家级自主创新示范区，围绕世界一流科技园区的总体目标，深入实施创新驱动、国际化提升和产城融合三大战略，在黄河流域科技创新与交流方面起到了重要的示范引领作用。

importance to the development of the Lan-Bai Self-innovation Zone, formulated a series of policy documents such as "Several Opinions on Supporting the Construction of Lanzhou-Baiyin National Independent Innovation Demonstration Zone" and "Opinions on Further Supporting the Lanzhou New Area to Deepen Reform and Innovation and Promote High-Quality Development", and established an innovation-driven policy system of "1+4+7" and "3+2+10". The Lan-Bai Fund was established to expand the attractiveness to social capital and a variety of fiscal policies were adopted to support the development of the Lan-Bai Self-innovation Zone. The two zones of Lan-Bai are closely following the forefront of national scientific and technological development, creating corporate innovation consortiums such as "Gansu Province Energy Equipment" and "Gansu Province Green Intelligent Highway Transportation"; around the fields of equipment manufacturing, information technology, bio-pharmaceuticals, etc., 22 provincial engineering research centers have been identified to integrate and create an innovative ecosystem. The Lanzhou Trade Fair and the Science and Technology Expo have attracted well-known Fortune 500 companies such as China National Biotech, Guangzhou Pharmaceutical Group, and Huawei Technologies to settle in the zone, enhancing the level of high-end industries in Gansu. In 2022, the regional gross product of the two Lan-Bai zones reached 123.3 billion yuan, accounting for more than 11% of the province's total, a 7% increase from the previous year; there were 759 high-tech enterprises, accounting for 45% of the province's total, gathering nearly 29% of the province's strategic emerging backbone enterprises and 41% of the listed companies. In addition, the Lan-Bai Self-innovation Zone fully utilized the characteristics of the Yellow River Basin region and actively connected with the Shanghai Zhangjiang National Independent Innovation Demonstration Zone. Both zones established working groups to jointly build platforms such as the Zhangjiang Lan-Bai Science and Technology Innovation Reform Pilot Zone Technology Transfer Center, and jointly organized events such as the "Lanzhou Science and Technology Expo" to carry out scientific research and achieve transformation of results. The two zones of Lan-Bai have also actively introduced high-quality innovative resources from Shanghai, Henan, Fujian, and other places to settle in Gansu, actively promoting the rapid application of a number of scientific and technological achievements in

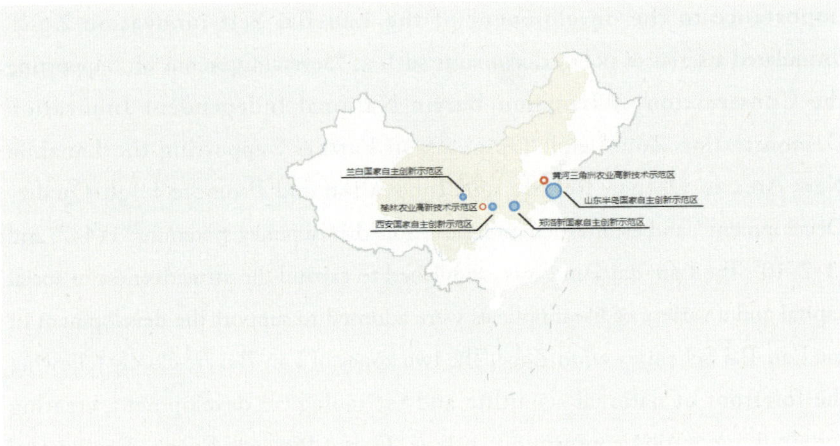

黄河流域国家自主创新示范区和农业高新技术示范区分布

Distribution of National Independent Innovation Demonstration Zone and Agricultural High-tech Demonstration Zone in the Yellow River Basin

西安国家自主创新示范区

Xi'an National Independent Innovation Demonstration Zone

the Lan-Bai New Area, such as the first domestic standard molten salt pump test device, reusable prevention and control masks, and low-temperature fiber paste application.

(2) Xi'an National Independent Innovation Demonstration Zone

The Xi'an National Independent Innovation Demonstration Zone (hereinafter referred to as "Xi'an Self-innovation Zone") was established in June 2015, located in Shaanxi Province in the middle reaches of the Yellow River. It is the first national-level independent innovation demonstration zone in the Yellow River Basin region. Focusing on the overall goal of a world-class science and technology park, it deeply implements three major strategies: innovation-driven, internationalization enhancement, and industry-city integration. It has played an important exemplary and leading role in scientific and technological innovation and exchange in the Yellow River Basin region.

The Xi'an Self-innovation Zone has accumulated a solid industrial and talent foundation over the years, with 49 research institutes, 311 key R&D platforms, and 186 new-type R&D institutions. Moreover, industry-leading companies such as Huawei and ZTE have established multiple R&D centers, and "stranglehold" technology industry clusters including artificial intelligence, aerospace, and new energy have gradually taken shape. In 2022, the Xi'an Self-innovation Zone newly identified 1,134 high-tech enterprises, bringing the total number of high-tech enterprises to 5,008. It added 4,607 new technology-based small and medium-sized enterprises, with the overall R&D intensity of the society reaching 7.5%, the contribution rate of scientific and technological progress reaching 75%, and the technical contract transaction volume reaching 110 billion yuan. The number of valid invention patents is 41,909, accounting for 58.5% of Xi'an City. It added 19 new national-level "little giant" enterprises, with a total of 57 in the zone, accounting for more than half of the city. It also added 56 new provincial-level "specialized, refined, and innovative" small and medium-sized enterprises, with a total of 279 in the zone, accounting for nearly two-thirds of the city. Xi'an Self-innovation Zone is well-versed in the art of talent cultivation, continuously introducing a series of talent attraction policies. It has simultaneously exerted efforts in areas such as funding, platforms, and projects, attracting more than 300 high-level talents and 600,000 science and technology professionals. This

西安自创区多年来积累下雄厚的产业和人才基础，拥有 49 家科研院所、311 个重点研发平台、186 家新型研发机构，更有华为、中兴等行业领先企业布局了多个研发中心，包含人工智能、航空航天、新能源等的“硬核”科技产业集群已逐渐形成。2022 年西安自创区新认定高新技术企业 1134 家，高新技术企业总量达到 5008 家，新增科技型中小企业 4607 家，全社会研发强度达到 7.5%，科技进步贡献率达到 75%，技术合同成交额达到 1100 亿元；有效发明专利拥有量 41909 件，占西安市 58.5%；新增国家级“小巨人”企业 19 家，全区累计达 57 家，占全市 1/2 以上。新增省级“专精特新”中小企业 56 家，全区累计达 279 家，占全市近 2/3。西安自创区深谙人才之道，接连出台多项人才吸引政策，在资金、平台、项目等多个方面同时发力，聚集高层次人才 300 余名、科技从业人员 60 万人，推动形成了“人才引领创新”的良好局面。西安自创区也逐渐探索出了一条校地、院地融合发展的新路子。例如，西安自创区与西北工业大学共同成立校地合作共建工作专班，致力于推动空天动力研究所、“秦创原”高能级科技成果转化平台建设。

（3）郑洛新国家自主创新示范区

郑洛新国家自主创新示范区（以下简称“郑洛新自创区”）是 2016 年经国务院审批成立的，由郑州、洛阳、新乡国家高新技术产业开发区组成的国家自主创新示范区。郑洛新自创区在深入推进高新技术产业和创新发展方面肩负着先行先试的引领作用，为黄河流域乃至全国的创新发展作出表率，对实现创新驱动与黄河流域高质量发展目标具有重要影响。

has fostered a favorable environment of "talent-led innovation". The Xi'an Self-innovation Zone has also gradually explored a new path of integration between universities and industries.For example, Xi'an Self-innovation Zone and Northwestern Polytechnical University jointly established a special working group for collaborative construction between universities and industries. They are committed to promoting the construction of the Aerospace Power Institute and the "Qinchuangyuan" high-level technology achievement transformation platform.

(3) Zhengzhou-Luoyang-Xinxiang National Independent Innovation Demonstration Zone

The Zhengzhou-Luoyang-Xinxiang National Independent Innovation Demonstration Zone (hereinafter referred to as "Zheng-Luo-Xin Self-innovation Zone") was established in 2016 with the approval of the State Council, composed of the national high-tech industrial development zones of Zhengzhou, Luoyang, and Xinxiang. The Zheng-Luo-Xin Self-innovation Zone plays a pioneering and leading role in deeply promoting high-tech industries and innovative development, setting an example for innovative development in the Yellow River Basin region and even the whole country, and has an important influence on achieving the goals of innovation-driven and high-quality development of the Yellow River Basin region.

The Zheng-Luo-Xin Self-innovation Zone focuses on the friendly interaction between industry and innovation, continuously coordinating the supply of various high-quality resources and optimizing the development environment. In terms of economic growth, the operating income of enterprises above designated size in the core area of the Zheng-Luo-Xin Self-innovation Zone in 2022 increased by 18.6% year-on-year, of which the high-tech manufacturing industry increased by 22.6% year-on-year, fully demonstrating the important driving role of scientific and technological innovation in regional economic development. In terms of innovation platform construction, several "national-level" innovation platforms, including the National Supercomputing Zhengzhou Center and the National Innovation Center for Biological Breeding Industry, have been established in the Zheng-Luo-Xin Self-innovation Zone. All kinds of high-quality resources gather in the self-innovation zone, and 15 industrial cluster projects of the self-innovation zone have been established and implemented, cultivating a number

郑洛新国家自主创新示范区

Zheng-Luo-Xin National Independent Innovation Demonstration Zone

郑洛新自创区注重产业与创新的友好互动，不断协调各项优质资源供给，优化发展环境。在经济增长方面，郑洛新自创区 2022 年核心区域的规模以上企业的营业收入同比增长 18.6%，其中高技术制造业同比增长了 22.6%，充分展示了科技创新对地区经济发展的重要驱动作用。在创新平台建设方面，多个“国字号”创新平台，包括国家超级计算郑州中心、国家生物育种产业创新中心等落地郑洛新自创区。各类优质资源齐聚自创区，设立并实施了 15 个自创区产业集群专项，培育形成了一批创新产业集群。截至 2022 年，自创区共拥有高新技术企业 3606 家，省级及以上创新载体超 1400 家，省级及以上重点实验室数量 109 家，科技孵化器 69 家，拥有院士工作站数量 100 多家。在创新成果方面，2022 年自创区核心区共获得专利授权量 20000 余件。8 个产业集群专项通过验收，累计申请专利 600 多项，部分项目填补了国内技术的空白。

of innovative industrial clusters. As of 2022, the self-innovation zone has a total of 3,606 high-tech enterprises, more than 1,400 provincial-level and above innovation carriers, 109 provincial-level and above key laboratories, 69 technology incubators, and more than 100 academician workstations. In terms of innovation achievements, the core area of the self-innovation zone obtained more than 20,000 patent authorizations in 2022. Eight industrial cluster projects have passed the acceptance, with a cumulative application of more than 600 patents, and some projects have filled the domestic technological gaps.

(4) Shandong Peninsula National Independent Innovation Demonstration Zone

The Shandong Peninsula National Independent Innovation Demonstration Zone (hereinafter referred to as "Shandong Peninsula Self-innovation Zone") was established in 2016, relying on the construction of six national high-tech industrial development zones in Jinan, Qingdao, Zibo, Weifang, Yantai, and Weihai of the Shandong Peninsula. It is the third national independent innovation demonstration zone in the Yellow River Basin region. The overall positioning is to be an independent innovation demonstration zone led by the blue economy to transform and upgrade, fully exerting the innovative resource advantages of the Shandong Peninsula, and building a marine science and technology innovation center with global influence.

In recent years, the six national high-tech zones of the Shandong Peninsula Self-innovation Zone have complemented and developed in conjunction, gradually opening up a pattern of technological innovation. In 2020, the "Jinan National Science and Technology Center" satellite was successfully launched, and the Quantum Technology Research Institute developed the world's first integrated multi-channel quantum frequency conversion chip. In 2021, it was approved to establish the only national-level graphene public technology service platform in northern China—the National Graphene Product Quality Supervision and Inspection Center (Shandong). The Shandong Peninsula Self-innovation Zone also closely revolves around the "dual carbon goals", and has built the country's first optical quantum radar atmospheric monitoring network by leveraging scientific and technological advantages, gradually realizing industrial application in the detection of pollutants and environmental haze control. The

济南高新技术产业开发区
Jinan National High-Tech Industrial Development Zone

（4）山东半岛国家自主创新示范区

山东半岛国家自主创新示范区（以下简称“山东半岛自创区）成立于2016年，依托山东半岛的济南、青岛、淄博、潍坊、烟台、威海六个国家高新技术产业开发区建设而成，是黄河流域第三家国家级自主创新示范区，总体定位是以蓝色经济引领转型升级的自主创新示范区，将山东半岛的创新资源优势充分发挥，打造具有全球影响力的海洋科技创新中心。

近年来，山东半岛自创区的六个国家高新区相互补充、联动发展，科技创新格局逐渐打开。2020年，“济南国科中心号”卫星成功发射，

development quality of the Shandong Peninsula Self-innovation Zone is steadily improving. Among them, Jinan High-tech Zone leads the Shandong Peninsula Self-innovation Zone. By the end of 2022, the total number of provincial-level research and development institutions in Jinan High-tech Zone has exceeded 280, the total number of listed enterprises in the zone has reached 122, the number of high-tech enterprises has exceeded 2,000, with 14 national-level technology business incubators, 34 national-level maker spaces and 4,214 incubating enterprises. Qingdao High-tech Industrial Development Zone follows closely. In 2022, it ranked 13th among national high-tech zones, rising 3 places from 16th in 2021. Its value-added of industrial enterprises above a designated size increased by 15.8% in 2022, and the total industrial output value increased by 14%. The general public budget revenue reached 3.506 billion yuan. It has nearly 40 innovation platforms at all levels, including 17 national-level incubators and innovation spaces, and more than 100 municipal-level or higher-level technology innovation centers and 18 municipal-level or higher-level new research and development institutions.

2. Agricultural High-tech Industrial Demonstration Zones

(1) Yangling Agricultural High-tech Industrial Demonstration Zone

As an important agricultural production area in the country, the quality of agricultural development in the Yellow River Basin region largely affects the national food security. The Yangling Agricultural High-tech Industrial Demonstration Zone (hereinafter referred to as "Yangling Demonstration Zone") is located in Shaanxi Province, in the Yellow River Basin region, and is the first national agricultural high-tech industrial demonstration zone in China. It undertakes the arduous tasks of biological engineering, breeding, and dryland agriculture in the Yellow River Basin region, playing a crucial role in the demonstration and dissemination of agricultural technology, as well as in external exchanges and cooperation.

Since its establishment in 1997, Yangling Demonstration Zone has fully utilized its advantages in agricultural science and education resources. Relying on research institutes such as Northwest A&F University and Shaanxi Hybrid Rapeseed Research Institute, it has continuously deepened cooperation between industry, academia, and research. The Yangling Demonstration Zone has more

量子技术研究院研制出国际首个集成化多通道量子频率转换芯片，2021年获批筹建中国北方唯一的国家级石墨烯公共技术服务平台——国家石墨烯产品质量监督检验中心（山东）。山东半岛自创区还紧紧围绕“双碳”目标，通过发挥科技优势，建成全国首张光量子雷达大气监测网，在污染物检测、环境治霾等方面逐步实现产业化应用。山东半岛自创区发展质量正稳步提升，其中，济南高新区领跑山东半岛自创区，截至2022年底，济南高新区省级研发机构总量累计突破280家，全区上市挂牌企业总数达到122家，高新技术企业突破2000家，拥有国家级科技企业孵化器14家，国家级众创空间达34家，在孵企业4214家。青岛高新技术开发区紧随其后，在2022年国家高新区中位列13名，较2021年第16名提升3个名次，2022年规上工业增加值增长15.8%，规上工业总产值增长14%，一般公共预算收入完成35.06亿元，拥有各级各类创新平台载体近40家，其中国家级孵化器、众创空间等达17家；拥有市级以上技术创新中心100余家、市级以上新型研发机构18家。

2. 农业高新技术产业示范区

（1）杨凌农业高新技术产业示范区

作为全国重要的农产品生产区，黄河流域的农业发展质量在很大程度上影响了全国的粮食安全。杨凌农业高新技术示范区（以下简称“杨凌示范区”）地处黄河流域的陕西省，是我国第一个国家农业高新技术产业示范区，肩负着黄河流域生物工程、育种、旱作农业等艰巨任务，在全国农业技术示范推广、对外合作交流等方面发挥着重要的推动作用。

than 40 research platforms at the provincial and ministerial levels. In 2022, the demonstration promotion area reached 110 million *mu*, with a total promotion benefit of 28.3 billion yuan. It has accumulated 350 demonstration promotion bases and has obtained national and provincial approval for 67 major crop varieties. The Yangling Demonstration Zone actively collaborates with advanced agricultural regions abroad. It has not only established a "1+3" international cooperation service platform in the agricultural sector but also focuses on the construction of the International Agricultural Innovation Port. Over ten research institutions, including the China-Kazakhstan Modern Research Center, have settled in the demonstration zone. The demonstration zone actively plays the role of government institutions, sets up promotion service departments according to local conditions, and adopts a variety of methods such as incentives and assessments to encourage promotion personnel to go deep into the front line, effectively solving the practical problems in the process of farmers' planting. The Yangling Demonstration Zone also focuses on improving the quality of farmers themselves, adopting a variety of measures such as the farmer technician system, expert demonstration, and farmers' professional cooperatives to accelerate the promotion of agricultural technology.

(2) Yellow River Delta Agricultural High-tech Demonstration Zone

The Yellow River Delta Agricultural High-tech Demonstration Zone (hereinafter referred to as "Yellow River Delta Agricultural High-tech Zone") is located in Dongying City, the lower reaches of the Yellow River Basin region. It is the second national agricultural high-tech industrial demonstration zone established in China. According to statistics, there are 104 million *mu* of saline-alkali land in the Yellow River Basin region, accounting for about 20% of the total saline-alkali land area in the country. Among them, the saline-alkali land characteristics in the Yellow River Delta region are particularly obvious, with a salinization degree of more than 80%, providing a natural experimental site for the development of modern agriculture on saline-alkali land.

杨凌智慧农业示范园（新华社记者张斌摄）
Yangling Smart Agriculture Demonstration Park (Photographed by Zhang Bin, Xinhua News Agency)

自 1997 年成立以来，杨凌示范区充分利用农科教资源优势，依托西北农林科技大学、陕西杂交油菜研究所等科研院所不断深化产学研合作，杨凌示范区拥有省部级以上研究平台 40 余个。2022 年示范推广面积 11000 万亩，推广总效益 283 亿元。累计示范推广基地 350 个。通过国审、省审主要农作物品种数量 67 个。杨凌示范区积极与国外农业先进地区展开合作，不仅在涉农领域搭建了“1+3”国际合作服务平台，而且注重国际农业创新港的建设，中国 - 哈萨克斯坦现代研究中心等十余家研究机构落户示范区。示范区积极发挥政府机构的作用，因地制宜设置推广服务部门，采取激励、考核等多种方式鼓励推广人员深入一线，切实解决农民种植过程中的实际问题。杨凌示范区也注重提升农民的自身素质，采取农民技术员制度、专家示范、农民专业合作社等多样

黄河三角洲农业高新技术示范区试验场

An Experimental Site in the Yellow River Delta Agricultural High-tech Demonstration Zone

It sounds like a "fabulous tale" to expect grain from land with a salt content as high as 6‰, but it has been preliminarily realized in the Yellow River Delta Agricultural High-tech Zone. The Yellow River Delta Agricultural High-tech Zone gathers high-quality scientific research resources from 34 universities including the Chinese Academy of Sciences, China Agricultural University, and Shandong Academy of Agricultural Sciences. It uses 440, 000 *mu* of coastal saline-alkali land to explore a unique path of comprehensive utilization of saline-alkali land for the whole country. Firstly, it has highlighted the development of specialty crops in saline-alkali land. The Yellow River Delta Agricultural High-Tech Zone has focused on constructing the Yellow River Delta National Seed Industry Innovation Industrial Park. It has collected more than 15,000 resources of salt-tolerant crops, strengthened the construction of the saline-alkali land specialty crop chain through breeding accelerators and integrated "breeding, propagation, and promotion". By introducing multiple breeding companies, it has formed a cluster of specialty industries for saline-alkali land. Secondly, it has

化措施，加速农业技术的推广。

（2）黄河三角洲农业高新技术示范区

黄河三角洲农业高新技术产业示范区（以下简称“黄三角农高区”），位于黄河流域下游的东营市，是我国设立的第二个国家农业高新技术产业示范区。据统计，黄河流域盐碱地面积有1.04亿亩，约占全国盐碱地总面积的20%，其中黄河三角洲地区土地盐碱化特征尤为明显，盐渍化程度高达80%以上，为发展盐碱地现代化农业提供了天然的试验场所。

向盐分高达6‰的土地要粮，听起来似乎是“天方夜谭”，但在黄三角农高区得以初步实现。黄三角农高区汇集中国科学院、中国农业大学、山东省农业科学院等34所高校和研究院的优质科研资源，利用44万亩滨海盐碱地，为全国探索出一条盐碱地综合利用特色路子。首先，突出发展了盐碱地特色种业。黄三角农高区以建设黄河三角洲国家种业创新产业园为重点，广泛收集盐生作物种资源1.5万余份，通过育种加速器，加强“育繁推”一体化的盐碱地特色种业链条建设，引进多家育种企业，形成了盐碱地特色产业集群。其次，着力促进高新技术产业的发展。以盐碱地特色种业为引领，重点培育了农业装备制造业、农业科技服务业等五大高新技术产业，同时依托生物技术研发平台，开发了北虫草等优质食品，研究并推广功能菌剂6.5万亩。最后，黄三角农高区还注重聚焦创新平台建设。利用无人机、大数据等现代化工具，为农业研发技术团队提供高效、准确的公共服务，用科技的翅膀助力黄河流域农业高质量发展。

三、智慧黄河建设

智慧黄河以人与自然和谐共生为理念，以让黄河成为造福人民的幸福河为目标，以新一代信息通信技术为主要驱动，用科技手段对黄河流

focused on promoting the development of high-tech industries. With saline-alkali land specialty crops as the leading factor, it has cultivated five major high-tech industries including agricultural equipment manufacturing and agricultural technology services. Additionally, relying on the biotechnology research and development platform, it has developed high-quality foods such as Northern Cordyceps and researched and promoted functional microbial agents on 65,000 *mu* of land. Finally, the Yellow River Delta Agricultural High-Tech Zone also emphasizes the construction of innovation platforms. Utilizing modern tools such as drones and big data, it provides efficient and accurate public services to agricultural research and development teams, empowering high-quality agricultural development in the Yellow River Basin with the wings of technology.

III. Construction of Smart Yellow River

The Smart Yellow River is guided by the concept of harmonious coexistence between humans and nature, aiming to make the Yellow River a river of happiness that benefits the people. Driven mainly by new-generation information and communication technology, it uses scientific and technological means for real-time monitoring and digital twin simulation of the water and sand conditions and human activities along the Yellow River Basin region, thereby achieving a new stage of transformation to a higher form of ecological protection and governance in the Yellow River Basin region.

1. "Clairaudience" and "Clairvoyance"

The development and utilization level of water resources in the Yellow River is as high as 80%, and water resources remain the greatest rigid constraint. The use of scientific and technological means for dynamic monitoring of the Yellow River's water environment, the current status and changes in the water-sand relationship, has endowed the Yellow River management with "clairaudience" and "clairvoyance". This not only targets the theme of ecological protection but is also an important part of high-quality development, helping to fundamentally transform the concept of Yellow River management and promote the coordinated development of ecological protection and high-quality development in the Yellow River Basin region.

域水沙状况及沿线人类活动进行实时监控并孪生模拟，从而实现黄河流域生态保护治理向更高级形态转型的新阶段。

1.“千里眼”与“顺风耳”

黄河水资源开发利用水平高达80%，水资源仍然是最大的刚性约束。运用科技手段动态监测黄河水环境、水沙关系现状与变化，为黄河治理赋予了“千里眼”与“顺风耳”。这不仅瞄准生态保护这一主题，也是高质量发展的重要一环，有助于促使黄河治理理念发生根本转变，协同推进黄河流域生态保护和高质量发展。

黄河流域在治理过程中综合利用多种新一代信息技术加强前端感知能力，并且注重数据中心建设，致力于构架天空地一体化生态资源环境监控体系，并积极推进数据信息进入“云端”，从而实现全面、动态、综合监控。黄河流域干线目前已有139个取水口、52个水土流失动态监测站点、逾1000路视频点在线实时监控，并构建了从黄河水利委员会至沿河基层单位的五级专用通信传输网络，不仅连接了黑河流域管理局和西北五省区网络，也将黄河流域下游78座引黄涵闸纳入其中，水利信息综合采集体系已基本形成。

黄河流域九省区在利用新一代信息技术监测治理方面纷纷做出自己的贡献。例如，内蒙古在2021年争取了水污染防治资金2.78亿元，建成多个黄河流域入河口监控平台；杭锦旗更是将“5G+智慧黄河”发挥得淋漓尽致，目前黄河杭锦旗段已完成23座云台、88个枪机、111路监控的规划与安装，利用360度旋转，300米可见的摄像机不仅能够全程、无死角、实时监控黄河的凌汛状况，也能对沿岸人工活动进行有效监控，对违法活动实现及时预警；山东省2021年黄河信息中心与其他单位联合申报多个研发项目，“基于多源图像的河道管理与监测平台”、

The Yellow River Basin has comprehensively utilized various new-generation information technologies to enhance its front-end perceptual capabilities during the governance process. It has also focused on the construction of data centers, aiming to build an integrated ecological resource and environmental monitoring system that spans the sky and the earth. Additionally, efforts have been made to actively promote the migration of data and information to the "cloud", thereby achieving comprehensive, dynamic, and integrated monitoring. Currently, there are 139 water intake points, 52 dynamic monitoring stations for soil and water erosion, and over 1000 online real-time video monitoring points along the main stream of the Yellow River. Furthermore, a five-level dedicated communication transmission network has been established from the Yellow River Conservancy Commission to grassroots units along the river. This network not only connects the Heihe River Basin Management Bureau and the five northwestern provinces and regions but also includes 78 Yellow River diversion sluice gates in the lower reaches of the Yellow River Basin into the system. As a result, a comprehensive water conservancy information collection system has been established.

The nine provinces and regions in the Yellow River Basin region have made their own contributions in utilizing new generation information technology for monitoring and governance. For example, Inner Mongolia secured 278 million yuan for water pollution prevention and control in 2021 and built multiple monitoring platforms at the river mouths of the Yellow River; Hangjin Banner has fully utilized "5G + Smart Yellow River", and has completed the planning and installation of 23 cloud platforms, 88 gun-type cameras, and 111 monitoring routes in the Hangjin Banner section of the Yellow River. Using cameras with 360-degree rotation and visibility of 300 meters, it can not only monitor the ice run status of the Yellow River in real time without dead angles but also effectively monitor human activities along the bank, providing timely warning for illegal activities. In 2021, the Yellow River Information Center of Shandong Province jointly applied for multiple research and development projects with other units. Among them, the "River Management and Monitoring Platform Based on Multi-source Images" and the "Holographic Fusion Tracking VR Panoramic Application Technology" were selected for inclusion in the Key Promotion and Guidance Catalog of Advanced and Practical Technologies by the Ministry of

"全息融合跟踪 VR 全景应用技术"入选水利部先进实用技术重点推广指导目录；德州市建立了生态黄河预警器，能够通过数字技术实现对排污、能耗状况实时监测；济南充分利用数据服务平台，加快数据要素流动，提高黄河大数据中心的建设进程。

2. 智慧大脑

（1）数字黄河

黄河流域信息化进程开端较早，自 2001 年 7 月以来，为实现新世纪治黄目标，黄河流域始终秉持着建立"原型黄河""数字黄河"和"模型黄河"科学决策场的目标，相继开展了水量统一调度、防汛泄洪统一指挥等项目。

"数字黄河"是利用现代信息技术采集并传输信息，构建黄河流域相关地区的经济、社会、环境等多要素数字化集成平台和虚拟环境，其关键作用在于提供快速科学的决策支持。"数字黄河"建设大致经过了三个阶段。2001—2007 年是"数字黄河"的一期建设阶段，在该阶段黄河流域编制规划报告，逐渐形成了一套完善的治理体系；提升网络通信水平，利用黄河高性能计算平台，初步形成了专业化的数学模型及应用开发；数据储存和技术服务体系基本搭建完成，"数字黄河"主体框架逐渐成形。2008—2012 年是"数字黄河"建设的第二阶段，在该阶段坚持建设"自然 - 经济 - 生态"耦合系统的目标，着力开展了六大类模型的研发工作，遥感技术的应用范围更加广泛，涉及防汛、污染治理、水土保持、水行政执法等多个领域，并成功创建了黄河地理空间信息共享服务原型平台。2013 年以来是"数字黄河"建设的第三阶段，也是"数字黄河"转型的攻坚阶段。目前已经完成了水资源监控、信息资源整合及共享等多个项目，"黄河一张图"绘制完成，大大提高了治理效率与能力，成功在水土流失治理、抗旱减灾、调水调沙等多个方面作出突出贡献，移动化、智能化成为黄河治理的新特征。

Water Resources. Dezhou City has established an ecological Yellow River early warning device, which can achieve real-time monitoring of pollution discharge and energy consumption status through digital technology; Jinan fully utilizes the data service platform to accelerate the flow of data elements and improve the construction process of the Yellow River Big Data Center.

2. Intelligent Brain

(1) Digital Yellow River

The informatization process of the Yellow River Basin region began relatively early. Since July 2001, to achieve the goals of Yellow River management in the new century, the Yellow River Basin region has always adhered to the goal of establishing a scientific decision-making field for the "prototype Yellow River" "digital Yellow River" and "model Yellow River", and has successively carried out projects such as unified water volume scheduling and unified command of flood control and flood discharge.

"Digital Yellow River" utilizes modern information technology to collect and transmit information, constructing a digital integrated platform and virtual environment for various elements such as economy, society, and environment in the Yellow River Basin region, with its key role being to provide rapid and scientific decision-making support. The construction of the "Digital Yellow River" has roughly gone through three stages. From 2001 to 2007, it was the first phase of construction for the "Digital Yellow River", during which the Yellow River Basin region formulated planning reports and gradually formed a comprehensive management system; improved network communication levels, using the Yellow River high-performance computing platform, initially formed specialized mathematical models and application development; the basic construction of data storage and technical service systems was completed, and the main framework of the "Digital Yellow River" gradually took shape. From 2008 to 2012, it was the second phase of the "Digital Yellow River" construction, during which the goal of building a "natural-economic-ecological" coupled system was adhered to, and efforts were made to develop six major types of models. The application range of remote sensing technology was further expanded, involving various fields such as flood control, pollution control, soil and water conservation, and water administrative law enforcement, and successfully created a prototype platform for

（2）数字孪生黄河

随着黄河流域生态保护和高质量发展国家战略的提出，黄河治理需要更加全面准确的监测信息和更高效的预警系统，“数字孪生黄河”成为黄河治理的新目标，能够为智慧黄河装上最强大脑。“数字孪生黄河”作为“数字黄河”的延续，能够通过数字映射、智能模拟、前瞻预演等功能与现实中的黄河同步仿真运行、虚实交互，从而能够更快速发现问题、做出决策、优化调度。

在“数字黄河”的基础上，“数字孪生黄河”开展了一系列的实践。在动态感知方面，实现了物联网与各类监测系统的联通，不仅能够展示水库、水文站的截面数据，还能查询各断面历年的冲淤时间序列数据；在预报调度方面，实现了气象预报数据与全链条业务模型的深度融合，能够预测黑石关、武陟等的径流量，基于相似度适配模型为小浪底水库选择最优调度方案；在方案预演方面，采用渲染插件的技术呈现出更高的渲染质量，克服了前期计算量大、渲染效率低的难题，能够实时为黄河下游洪水过程中居民撤退迁安生成最优线路，并进行洪水演进方案预演展示，为防汛防洪提供最科学的支持。《数字孪生黄河建设规划(2022—2025)》的出台为“数字孪生黄河”提出了新的建设目标。规划指出，“十四五”时期，黄河流域要初步建成“2+N”智能应用体系，继续提升流域数字化、网络化水平，将数字孪生成果接入小浪底、万家寨等重要水库。2022年水利部紧密部署了94项数字孪生流域（水利工程）先行先试建设任务，小浪底被列为数字孪生先行先试头号工程，自2022年3月以来，历经1年多的开发建设，数字孪生小浪底已具雏形。未来“数字孪生黄河”不仅仅是一种通用技术，也将成为大家发现、认知、改造黄河的新方式。

sharing Yellow River geospatial information services. Since 2013, it has been the third phase of the "Digital Yellow River" construction and also a key stage in its transformation. Several projects such as water resource monitoring, integration and sharing of information resources have been completed, and the "Yellow River Map" has been drawn, greatly improving the efficiency and capability of management. It has made outstanding contributions in various aspects such as soil erosion control, drought resistance and disaster reduction, and water and sediment regulation. Mobility and intelligence have become new characteristics of Yellow River management.

(2) Digital Twin of the Yellow River

With the introduction of the national strategy for ecological protection and high-quality development in the Yellow River Basin region, Yellow River management requires more comprehensive and accurate monitoring information and a more efficient early warning system. The "Digital Twin of the Yellow River" has become a new goal for Yellow River management, capable of equipping the smart Yellow River with the most powerful brain. The "Digital Twin of the Yellow River", as a continuation of the "Digital Yellow River", can synchronize with the real Yellow River in simulation operation and virtual interaction through digital mapping, intelligent simulation, and forward preview, thus being able to discover problems more quickly, make decisions, and optimize scheduling.

On the basis of the "Digital Yellow River", the "Digital Twin of the Yellow River" has carried out a series of practices. In terms of dynamic perception, it has achieved the connection between the Internet of Things and various monitoring systems, not only displaying the cross-sectional data of reservoirs and hydrological stations but also querying the sedimentation time series data of various sections over the years. In terms of forecasting and scheduling, the deep integration of meteorological forecast data with the full-chain business model has been achieved, which can predict the runoff of Heishiguan, Wuzhi, etc., and select the optimal scheduling plan for the Xiaolangdi Reservoir based on the similarity adaptation model. In terms of plan rehearsal, the use of rendering plug-in technology presents higher rendering quality of results, overcoming the difficulties of large amount of early calculation and low rendering efficiency. It can generate the optimal route for residents to retreat and relocate during the flood process in the

黄河实验室数字孪生黄河工场

Digital Twin Yellow River Workshop of the Yellow River Laboratory

3. 东数西算

"东数西算"工程是继"南水北调""西电东送""西气东输"三大资源调配工程之后的又一重大战略部署，通过构建新型算力网络体系，利用西部地区充裕的土地资源和可再生能源，发展数据中心，承接东部算力需求。黄河流域数字化发展离不开其强大的数据处理与计算能力，"东数西算"是其强大算力的有力证明。同时，"东数西算"工程涉及设备制造、基础软件、绿色能源等多个领域，其产业链条长、投资规模大、技术要求高，对地区经济和上下游产业的发展具有显著的带动作用，"东数西算"不仅能够推动电子信息制造业、信息通信业等多产业的战略布局，还能带动云计算、物联网、区块链等新兴技术在黄河流域生根发芽。黄河流域生态算力中心已经启动建设，将推动以生态保护、气象水文、智能 AI 等对算力有刚性需求的"东数西算"典型示范场景的搭建，实现流域生态环境监管数字化转型。

lower reaches of the Yellow River in real time, and carry out the rehearsal and display of the flood evolution plan, providing the most scientific support for flood prevention and flood control. The "Digital Twin of the Yellow River Construction Plan (2022-2025)" has set new construction goals for the "Digital Twin of the Yellow River". The plan points out that during the "14th Five-Year Plan" period, the Yellow River Basin region should initially build a "2+N" intelligent application system, continue to improve the level of digitalization and networking of the Yellow River Basin, and connect the achievements of digital twins to important reservoirs such as Xiaolangdi and Wanjiazhai. In 2022, the Ministry of Water Resources closely arranged 94 pilot construction tasks for digital twin basins (water conservancy projects), with Xiaolangdi being listed as the top pilot project for digital twins. Since March 2022, after more than a year of development and construction, the digital twin of Xiaolangdi has taken shape. In the future, the "Digital Twin of the Yellow River" will not only be a general technology but also a new way for everyone to discover, understand, and transform the Yellow River.

3. East Data, West Computing

The East Data West Computing Project is another major strategic deployment following the three major resource allocation projects of "South-to-North Water Diversion" "West-to-East Electricity Transmission" and "West-to-East Gas Transmission". It develops data centers by building a new type of computing power network system, utilizing the abundant land resources and renewable energy in the western region to meet the computing power demands of the eastern region. The digital development of the Yellow River Basin region is inseparable from its powerful data processing and computing capabilities, and "East Data, West Computing" is a strong testament to its computing power. At the same time, the East Data West Computing Project involves multiple fields such as equipment manufacturing, basic software, and green energy. It has a long industrial chain, large investment scale, and high technical requirements, which significantly drives the development of regional economies and upstream and downstream industries. The East Data West Computing Project can not only promote the strategic layout of multiple industries such as electronic information manufacturing and information communication services, but also foster the growth of emerging technologies like cloud computing, the Internet of Things,

国家超级计算郑州中心

National Super-Computing Center (Zhengzhou)

四、新路径优化

1. 现存问题

（1）创新水平有待进一步提升

近年来，黄河流域科技创新水平显著提升，但仍存在进步空间。首先，在创新资源方面，黄河流域不仅与京津冀、长三角、粤港澳大湾区等地区有较大差距，且与整体长江经济带相比也有诸多不足。《中国区域创新能力评价报告 2022》显示，黄河流域创新能力低于全国创新能力

and blockchain in the Yellow River Basin region. The construction of the Yellow River Basin region ecological computing power center has been initiated, which will promote the establishment of typical demonstration scenarios of "East Data, West Computing" with rigid demand for computing power, such as ecological protection, meteorological hydrology, and intelligent AI, achieving the digital transformation of the Yellow River Basin's ecological environment supervision.

IV. New Path Optimization

1.Existing Problems

(1) Need for Further Improvement in the Level of Innovation

In recent years, the level of scientific and technological innovation in the Yellow River Basin region has been significantly improved, but there is still room for progress. Firstly, in terms of innovation resources, there is a significant gap between the Yellow River Basin region and regions such as the Beijing-Tianjin-Hebei area, the Yangtze River Delta, and the Guangdong-Hong Kong-Macao Greater Bay Area, and there are also many deficiencies compared to the overall Yangtze River Economic Belt. According to the "China Regional Innovation Capability Evaluation Report 2022", the innovation capability of the Yellow River Basin region is below the national average, with Ningxia, Gansu, and Inner Mongolia ranking among the bottom five regions in terms of innovation capability in China. The gap between the Yellow River Basin region and high-innovation areas is not only evident in the talent pool and R&D investment but also in terms of top-level design, innovation coordination mechanisms, and other aspects of the innovation ecosystem. There are also deficiencies in explicit indicators such as research institutions, innovation outcomes, and technology funding.

(2) Lack of a Strong Core Growth Pole and Innovation-driven Axis

The rapid growth of a regional economy is inseparable from a strong growth pole. Although the Yellow River Basin region has preliminarily formed economic circles and city clusters such as the Jinan Economic Circle, the Central Plains city cluster, and the Guanzhong city cluster with certain scientific and economic strength, there is still a big gap compared with the Yangtze River Economic

均值，尤其是宁夏、甘肃和内蒙古三省（区）的创新能力位于我国后五位。同时，黄河流域与创新高地的差距不仅仅体现在人才队伍、研发投入，在顶层设计、创新协调机制等创新生态、科研机构、创新成果、技术资金等显性指标方面也存在短板与不足。

（2）缺乏强大的核心增长极和创新驱动轴线

一个区域经济的快速增长离不开实力强大的增长极。尽管黄河流域已初步形成具有一定科技经济实力的济南经济圈、中原城市群与关中城市群，但与长江经济带的长三角城市群、成渝城市群等相比还存在很大的差距。例如，同为省会城市的郑州和武汉相比，2022 年武汉 GDP 约为 18866.43 亿元，郑州 GDP 约为 12934.7 亿元，二者相差约 5931.73 亿，武汉有 13 个市辖区，常住人口超过 1373.90 万，建成区面积近 1217 平方千米，而郑州只有 6 个市辖区，常住人口为 1282.8 万人，城市建成区面积为 689 平方千米。这也从侧面说明了现有城市群辐射力无法覆盖整个黄河流域，难以在流域的经济发展中起到有效的统领作用，更承担不了带领黄河流域参与全国甚至全球分工与竞争的重任。

（3）黄河流域科技创新协同水平不高

黄河流域不仅整体科技创新水平与能力较为薄弱，而且区域间协同水平有待进一步增强。首先，黄河流域科技创新水平总体呈现“东强西弱”的格局，整体差异较大。东部省份的科技创新能力排名较靠前，而中西部省区的科技创新水平较为落后。第二，由于开发主体利益不同，多数省区仅考虑自身发展需求，整体观念不足，创新溢出效应有待增加。第三，黄河流域缺乏强有力的科技创新协同推进政策。目前，黄河流域尚未形成涉及全流域的科技创新协调机制，区域间科技合作机制有待健全。

2. 未来发展方向

（1）统筹科技创新规划，增强开放联动效应

立足于黄河流域不同地区的资源禀赋和发展特点，编制黄河流域科

Belt's Yangtze River Delta city cluster and Chengdu-Chongqing city cluster. For example, as a provincial capital city, Wuhan's GDP is about 1886.643 billion in 2022, while Zhengzhou's GDP is about 1293.47 billion, with a gap of about 593.173 billion between the two. Wuhan has 13 municipal districts, a permanent population of more than 13.739 million, and a built-up area of nearly 1217 square kilometers, while Zhengzhou only has 6 municipal districts, a permanent population of 12.828 million people, and an urban built-up area of 689 square kilometers. This also indirectly indicates that the existing city clusters' radiating power cannot cover the entire Yellow River Basin region, making it difficult to play an effective leading role in the economic development of the basin, let alone take on the heavy responsibility of leading the Yellow River Basin region to participate in national and even global division of labor and competition.

(3) Low level of the Collaborative Level of Sci-tech Innovation in the Yellow River Basin Region

The Yellow River Basin region not only has a relatively weak overall level and capability of scientific and technological innovation, but also the level of regional collaboration needs to be further enhanced. Firstly, the level of scientific and technological innovation in the Yellow River Basin region generally shows a pattern of "strong east and weak west", with significant overall differences. The eastern provinces rank higher in scientific and technological innovation capabilities, while the central and western provinces and regions are relatively backward in scientific and technological innovation levels. Secondly, due to different interests of development entities, most provinces and regions only consider their own development needs, lacking a holistic concept, and the innovation spillover effect needs to be increased. Thirdly, the Yellow River Basin region lacks strong policies for promoting scientific and technological innovation collaboration. At present, the Yellow River Basin region has not yet formed a scientific and technological innovation coordination mechanism involving the entire basin, and the mechanism for inter-regional scientific and technological cooperation needs to be improved.

2. Future Development Directions

(1) To Coordinate Sci-tech Innovation Planning to Enhance the Effect of Opening-up Linkage

技创新规划，以此来整合全流域科技创新资源，统筹沿黄各省区的经济布局，构建优势互补、互利共赢的黄河流域发展新格局。同时，推动实施一批具有前瞻性、全局性和带动性的科研项目，布局建设一批科技成果转移基地，加快“数字孪生黄河”建设，全面提升全流域生态治理和经济发展的信息化和智能化水平，这对于充分发挥科技对黄河流域生态保护和高质量发展的支撑作用具有重要影响。

（2）加大科技创新投入，激发创新主体动力

首先，完善科技投融资机制。尝试采取“政府＋银行＋保险”三方合作的形式，对贷款保费和损失赔偿给予适当的财政补贴，对黄河流域企业技术创新活动提供持续资金支持。其次，放大财政资金创新支持效应。建立财政科技投入稳定增长机制，确保财政科技投入增长幅度高于财政经常性收入增长幅度；充分发挥创业投资引导基金的作用，形成财政资金和社会资本合力创新的研发经费投入格局；集中财力加大对事关黄河流域生态保护和高质量发展的重大科技项目实施、共性关键技术攻关等领域的支持力度。最后，支持鼓励科技型企业创新发展，对创新能力强、发展前景好的初创期科技型企业给予资金支持。

Based on the resource endowment and development characteristics of different regions in the Yellow River Basin region, a scientific and technological innovation plan for the Yellow River Basin region will be formulated to integrate scientific and technological innovation resources across the entire basin, coordinate the economic layout of the provinces and regions along the Yellow River, and build a new pattern of development for the Yellow River Basin region that complements each other's advantages and achieves mutual benefit and win-win results. At the same time, promote the implementation of a number of scientific research projects with forward-looking, overall, and driving significance. Also, plan and build a number of bases for the transfer of scientific and technological achievements, accelerate the construction of the "Digital Twin of the Yellow River", and comprehensively improve the level of informatization and intelligence of ecological governance and economic development in the entire basin. This exerts an important impact on giving full play to the supporting role of science and technology in the ecological protection and high-quality development of the Yellow River Basin region.

(2) To Increase Investment in Sci-tech Innovation to Stimulate the Motivation of Innovation Entities

Firstly, improve the scientific and technological investment and financing mechanism. Try to adopt a tripartite cooperation model of "government + bank + insurance", provide appropriate financial subsidies for loan premiums and loss compensation. Provide continuous financial support for technological innovation activities of enterprises in the Yellow River Basin region. Secondly, amplify the innovative support effect of fiscal funds. Establish a stable growth mechanism for fiscal scientific and technological investment to ensure that the growth rate of fiscal scientific and technological investment is higher than the growth rate of fiscal regular income; give full play to the role of venture investment guiding funds, and form a pattern of research and development funding investment that combines fiscal funds and social capital; concentrate financial resources to increase support for major scientific and technological projects related to ecological protection and high-quality development of the Yellow River Basin region, and key common technical problems. Finally, support and encourage the innovative development of technology enterprises, and provide financial support to

（3）成立黄河流域科技创新联盟，加快培育新兴增长极

成立黄河流域科技创新联盟，将会充分发挥黄河横跨多个省区的纽带作用，合力打造高能级科技创新平台，高效促进相关领域高质量技术成果的转移转化，实现更高水平的交流互动，促进我国东中西部科技经济的交流和融合发展。因此，黄河流域九省区要把提高黄河流域生态保护的原始创新能力摆在更加突出的位置，围绕“凝心聚力，共谋发展”“同抓保护，共促发展”“资源共享，合作发展”“产业为基，支撑发展”四个方面凝心聚力开展科技合作，加快科技成果的转化与应用，为黄河流域高质量发展提供“新路子”和“新举措”，还可以揭榜挂帅的方式，开展诸如黄河乌兰布和沙漠段风沙防治和退化土地治理关键技术及其产业化、焦化废水零排放与分盐资源化利用、高品质金刚石合成智能化装备关键技术开发、电子级多晶硅材料关键制备技术等方面的研究。

综上所述，“十四五”是推动黄河流域生态保护和高质量发展的关键时期，要实现高质量发展目标，必须依靠创新驱动的内涵型增长，即要以科技创新催生新发展动能。回首过去，黄河流域凭借丰富的创新资源和巨大的创新潜力，在创新人才引进、创新平台建设、数字技术运用等多个方面都取得了显著的成就。展望未来，黄河流域需要在巩固现有创新成果的基础上，持续深入实施创新驱动发展战略，加大科技创新投入力度，加强新旧动能转换，以科技创新助力更高水平的高质量发展。

technology enterprises with strong innovation capabilities and good development prospects in their early stages.

(3) To Establish the Yellow River Basin Region Science and Technology Innovation Alliance to Accelerate the Cultivation of Emerging Growth Poles

Establishing the Yellow River Basin region Science and Technology Innovation Alliance will fully utilize the role of the Yellow River as a link across multiple provinces and regions. Jointly create a high-energy scientific and technological innovation platform, efficiently promote the transfer and transformation of high-quality technical achievements in related fields, achieve a higher level of exchange and interaction, and promote the exchange and integrated development of science and technology economy in the eastern, central, and western regions of our country. Therefore, the nine provinces and regions of the Yellow River Basin region must put the improvement of the original innovation capability for ecological protection in the Yellow River Basin region in a more prominent position, unite and work together in scientific and technological cooperation around the four aspects of "uniting efforts and seeking common development", "focusing on protection and promoting development together", "sharing resources and developing through cooperation", and "industry as the foundation, supporting development", accelerate the transformation and application of scientific and technological achievements, and provide "new approaches" and "new measures" for high-quality development in the Yellow River Basin region. Research can also be carried out in a "ranking leadership" manner on key technologies for wind and sand control and degraded land management in the Ulan Buh Desert section of the Yellow River and their industrialization, zero discharge and resource utilization of coking wastewater, development of key technologies for intelligent equipment of high-quality diamond synthesis, and key preparation technologies for electronic-grade polysilicon materials.

In summary, the "14th Five-Year Plan" period is a key period for promoting ecological protection and high-quality development in the Yellow River Basin region. To achieve the goals of high-quality development, it is essential to rely on innovation-driven connotation growth, that is, to generate new drivers of development through scientific and technological innovation. Looking back, the Yellow River Basin region has made significant achievements in various

aspects such as the introduction of innovative talents, the construction of innovation platforms, and the application of digital technology, thanks to its abundant innovation resources and tremendous innovation potential. Looking forward, the Yellow River Basin region needs to build on the existing innovation achievements, continue to implement the innovation-driven strategy in depth, increase investment in scientific and technological innovation, strengthen the transformation of old and new kinetic energy conversion, and promote higher levels of high-quality development with scientific and technological innovation.